Anonymus

The Life and Times of Leo the Tenth

Anonymus

The Life and Times of Leo the Tenth

ISBN/EAN: 9783743341586

Manufactured in Europe, USA, Canada, Australia, Japa

Cover: Foto ©ninafisch / pixelio.de

Manufactured and distributed by brebook publishing software (www.brebook.com)

Anonymus

The Life and Times of Leo the Tenth

THE

LIFE AND TIMES

OF

LEO THE TENTH.

LONDON:
THE RELIGIOUS TRACT SOCIETY;
Instituted 1799.

CONTENTS.

	Page
CHAPTER I.	5
CHAPTER II.	17
CHAPTER III.	28
CHAPTER IV.	43
CHAPTER V.	55
CHAPTER VI.	66
CHAPTER VII.	81
CHAPTER VIII.	97
CHAPTER IX.	109
CHAPTER X.	119
CHAPTER XI.	135
CHAPTER XII.	150
CHAPTER XIII.	165
CHAPTER XIV.	180

THE LIFE AND TIMES

OF

LEO THE TENTH.

CHAPTER I.

Decline of the imperial, and growth of the papal power—Rise of the German empire—The pope subject to the emperor—Becomes an independent sovereign — Arrogance of the papacy in the middle ages—Strifes of the Guelfs and Ghibelines—Consequent state of Italy, and especially of Florence—Feuds and free spirit of the Florentines—The Medici family—Cosmo de' Medici—Lorenzo the Magnificent.

WHEN the sun of the ancient Roman grandeur declined in the west, it made a feeble and transient effort to rise again in the east. The seat of government was transferred from Rome to Constantinople by the emperor Constantine, in the hope that the richer part of the empire might thus be secured from the encroaching hordes of barbarians who threatened its eastern and northern frontiers. This step, though perhaps unavoidable, exposed Italy to the incursions of those tribes which had already passed the Danube and the Rhine, and only waited a favourable opportunity to cross the Alps, and fix their habitations on the banks of the Po and its tributary streams. Accordingly, in the spring of the year 568, the fierce Lombard chief Alboin, with 20,000 followers, bade farewell to his possessions in Pannonia, now part of Hungary, and descended on that extensive and well-watered plain, to which his conquest has given the perpetual name of Lombardy. No Roman army opposed his march, for the spirit of the Romans was well nigh extinct, and the provinces of Italy which yet remained to the empire were distracted by mutual dissensions. Rome was only occasionally the seat of government; for the exarch, or deputy governor, quite as often chose the rising sea-port Ravenna for his place of abode, because of the facilities it afforded for communication with the imperial court.

Thus it happened that the bishop of Rome, whose authority had hitherto been wholly of a spiritual kind, but whose influential position and constantly increasing wealth gave him precedence even of the greatest nobles, easily and almost naturally became the political as well as ecclesiastical head of the city and its dependent territory. By his means it was that the Lombard invaders, who professed the Christian faith, were induced to respect the possessions, and to enter into a league with the people of Rome.

This alteration, however, in the functions and character of the popedom, was pregnant with results momentous to the destinies of Europe, and disastrous to the remaining purity of the church. Previously, indeed, the bishops of Rome had made alarming advances in luxury and worldly pomp, but the lust of power was now added to their former vices, and they soon learned to use religion only as an instrument of state policy and self-aggrandizement.

As the ancient empire thus crumbled into ruins, another arose in Western Europe, that eventually comprehended nearly all the fragments of which the Roman had been composed. The foundations of this new empire were laid by the earliest French kings, but the work of erecting it was carried on most rapidly towards the close of the eighth century, by Pepin and his son Charlemagne. Both Pepin and Charlemagne were zealous upholders of the pope's prerogatives. It is related, that Astolphus, the king of the Lombards, having captured Ravenna, laid siege to Rome, when the pontiff, Stephen III., besought the assistance of Pepin. The French monarch routed the Lombards, and was then requested to restore Ravenna to the emperor, to whom, in justice, it belonged. Pepin's reply discovered his superstitious awe of the pope's authority: "For no favour of man have I entered into this strife, but from veneration to St. Peter alone, and in the hope of obtaining the forgiveness of my sins." He then caused the keys of all the towns he had conquered to be laid on the altar of St. Peter's, in token of the pope's right to the sovereign power. His son Charlemagne showed the same deference for the papal authority. Having entirely conquered Lombardy, he visited Rome, where he was received with great rejoicings, as a friend and ally. A procession of Roman youths of noble birth met him at a distance from the city, bearing crosses and ensigns of the saints. At the sight of the sacred emblems, Charles dismounted from his horse, and entering the gates at the head of his soldiers, proceeded to the Vatican, where he was awaited by the pope, Adrian I. Ascending the stairs, the king devoutly kissed each step, until he crossed "the threshold of the apostles," as it was styled. The pope, surrounded by his cardinals, received him in great state, and gave him his paternal benediction. Charles continued his victorious career, and in the year 800, when a large part of Europe was subject to his sway, he was solemnly crowned by pope Leo III. as Cæsar Augustus. He afterwards confirmed to the papacy all the possessions which Pepin had bestowed. "Thus," says Gibbon, "the world beheld, for the first time, a Christian bishop invested with the prerogatives of a temporal prince; the choice of magistrates, the exercise of justice, the imposition of taxes, and the wealth of the palace of Ravenna."

But, although the pope was thus created a temporal prince, he was not regarded as wholly independent. As he received his dominion from the emperor, so he was considered responsible to that monarch for the proper use of his power; his estates were reckoned as an integral part of the empire; and when the sceptre was wrested from him by death, it was placed in the hands of a successor approved, if not selected, by the emperor. Even when the empire itself passed away from the immediate descendants of Charlemagne, and became the possession of the German house, the relation between the pope and the emperor continued unchanged. In all political matters the supremacy of the latter was maintained and acknowledged. In the tenth century, Otho the Great, who proved himself, on many occasions, a zealous friend of the papal interests, by patronising eminent men among the clergy, and by endowing abbeys and convents, nevertheless always asserted his sovereign right, both in the election of the popes, and in superintending their temporal affairs. No election, indeed, was regarded as valid till after the ceremony of investiture, in which the episcopal staff and ring were solemnly presented to the bishop elect by the hands of the emperor.

But it was impossible that these restrictions should long continue to fetter the growing power of the papal church. Even in the time of Otho the Great, her possessions had so increased that ecclesiastical estates were no longer described as situated in certain counties, but the counties themselves were denominated as parts of particular bishoprics. And while this church was advancing in wealth and influence, the empire was declining in both. It was one necessary consequence of the feudal system, which then flourished in Europe, that there should grow up in each country a numerous and powerful nobility, able at any time, by combining, to overthrow the supreme authority and establish another. In Northern Italy, many of the nobles had renounced their allegiance to the empire, and established themselves as petty sovereigns, or as leaders in civic republics. The pope was not far behind in this race for power.

In the year 1073, the tiara was placed on the brows of a man whose ambitious and resolute character well fitted him to assert the independence of the papal crown. This was Hildebrand, who assumed the title of Gregory VII. The imperial throne was then filled by Henry IV. of Germany. The pope's first act was to publish an edict, everywhere depriving the laity of the right to confer any clerical office, which evidently was equivalent to forbidding the emperor his ancient prerogative of the investiture. He next ventured to accuse the emperor of violating this decree in some inferior instances, and haughtily commanded him to come to Rome to apologize; asserting that "the pope is through God, and instead of God on earth, therefore all powers are subject to him. The pope is the sun, the emperor the moon that shines with borrowed light!" Henry, conscious of weakness, was at first anxious to conciliate the arrogant priest, and that he might do so, actually crossed the snow-covered Alps, in the depth of a very severe winter, taking with him also his queen and infant son. On reaching the castle of Canossa, a fortress in the bosom of the Apennines, where Gregory was residing, he was ordered to enter the castle-yard alone, on foot, and in the habit of a penitent. Henry obeyed; and had no sooner entered than the gates were closed behind him, and for three days and nights he remained there, without food, bare-headed and bare-footed, exposed in a woollen garment to the piercing winter's cold. At length, Gregory consented to an interview, and Henry, after undergoing every species of humiliation, received a kind of absolution, and was dismissed by the triumphant pope. It is impossible to contemplate such a scene without the saddest emotions. Here is a minister of religion, a professed follower of the meek and lowly Jesus, claiming to be the pattern and teacher of all others, yet displaying a degree of pride and malice that we shall hardly find paralleled in history. Here is a so-called ordinance of religion, that of penance, perverted into the mere tool of a prelate's pride, and provoking the mockery of every unbeliever. A church whose chief officer was a living contradiction of its principal doctrines, was evidently ripening for destruction.

Indignant at the treatment he had received, the emperor nominated the archbishop of Ravenna as pope, and formally invested him by the title of Clement III. Gregory excommunicated Henry, and as the hereditary iron crown of the empire was in Henry's possession, crowned with a new diadem a Swabian noble, who had already usurped the imperial title. Thus pope was opposed to pope, and emperor to emperor.

Here commenced the celebrated strife of the Guelfs, or partisans of the pope, and the Ghibbelines, or adherents to the emperor—a strife which rent into fierce factions the whole population of Germany and Italy, and continued in the latter country long after the original dispute was settled and nearly forgotten. For as the emperors, engrossed by their German affairs, relaxed their hold upon Italy, the names of Guelf and Ghibbeline gained a new meaning, and the struggle became one of personal or municipal ambition among the Italians themselves—the Ghibbelines being generally animated by a spirit of aristocracy, and the Guelfs being the favourers of a popular form of government.

Such was for centuries the unquiet state of Northern Italy, and in particular of FLORENCE, the city which gave birth to LEO X. This city was so favourably situated for the pursuits of commerce, and had entered into them with so much vigour, as to stand foremost among the great towns of Italy for wealth and grandeur; so that it has, not unworthily, been styled "the metropolis of the middle ages." Its government was republican—a form which, with many important faults, is well adapted to afford encouragement to all descriptions of enterprise and talent. Accordingly, there were numerous families in Florence that had risen to distinction by their own exertions, and were often competitors for the most illustrious offices in the state. Her very constitution was thus so favourable to the spirit of faction, that it is no matter of surprise that, after the conflicts of Guelf and Ghibbeline had ended, a personal squabble should have arrayed the same parties against each other, under the names of Neri and Bianchi, the black and the white. Of these unhappy divisions the Florentine poet Dante often complains in his poem, the "Divina Commedia," blaming the Ghibbelines, or aristocrats, for abusing the power of the state to party purposes, and the Guelfs for revolting from legitimate authority, though oppressively used. He says:—

"These 'gainst the public banner do array
   The yellow lilies; those a partisan
   Would make it;—which most wrong 'twere hard to say.
Let, let the Ghibbelines pursue their arts
   Beneath some other ensign, for accurst
   Is he who *it* and *equity* disparts."

He might well speak bitterly, for he was himself a principal sufferer, having been banished from the city A.D. 1297, together with the whole of the Bianchi party, whose interests he had espoused.

The spirit of independence, however, which so disturbed the peace of the city with these fierce affrays, was at the same time favourable to free competition in the pursuits of science and art, and Florence was illumined with the first rays that broke upon the gloom of the mediæval night.

No family distinguished itself more honourably in the patronage of letters than that of the MEDICI, which for ages was esteemed among the most considerable in the republic. This family had risen to great wealth by diligently prosecuting the trade with India and the east, which, before the discovery of the passage by the Cape of Good Hope, flowed into Europe chiefly by way of Egypt, through the Italian republics, Venice and Genoa. Of these republics Florence ultimately became a successful and flourishing rival.

For several generations the Medici family had been increasing in opulence and public esteem, but Giovanni de' Medici, who lived in the fourteenth century, may perhaps be considered as having laid the foundation of the greatness attained by his posterity. His son Cosmo trod carefully in his father's footsteps, and acquired so much wealth and political influence as to excite the jealousy of his fellow-citizens, who banished him for ten years, merely lest he should use his power to the detriment of the state. He took a noble and patriotic revenge, by travelling through the cities of Italy to purchase rare manuscripts and works of art, with which, on his return, he enriched his native town. In the erection of many splendid buildings for public use, in patronising learned and scientific men, in collecting relics of antiquity and the beautiful productions of contemporary artists, Cosmo expended immense sums of money; and having lived for many years in the enjoyment of the highest esteem, he left behind him the character of a public benefactor, and even before his death was honoured, by decree of the citizens, with the title of "Father of his country."

The grandson of Cosmo was now sixteen years old, and after an interval of four years was acknowledged, A.D. 1468, as a worthy successor to his grandsire's estates, and to the influential position he held in the republic; for although the form of government forbade any hereditary succession to the offices of state, yet it could not but happen, in so small a population, that those who had the greatest wealth, and the most numerous and powerful connexions abroad, should always have much weight in the councils at home, and be able for the most part to regulate at their pleasure the acts of the government. This was precisely the position occupied formerly by Cosmo, and now by Lorenzo de' Medici, afterwards called the Magnificent. He not only took the place of his grandfather, but very greatly surpassed him in his love of learning and the arts, as well as in possessing a genius that conducted him to excellence of the first order in statesmanship, and to no mean degree of merit in poetry and other literary pursuits. His influence as a statesman was felt in all the governments that were' then established, and he is usually regarded as the first who aimed at preserving a due balance of power among the European states. Under his auspices, Florence rose high in the political scale, notwithstanding her natural inferiority. He, like his grandfather, spared no cost in embellishing the city. He adorned her squares and streets with stately palaces; his country houses and gardens exhibited the utmost refinement of taste, and were so freely the resort of the ingenious and the learned, that they might, not inaptly, be designated the nursery of the infant arts. He zealously collected specimens of ancient art, and manuscripts of the Greek and Latin classics, whilst he was one of the first to patronise the invention of printing, which contributed so largely to the revival of letters. It is saddening to reflect that, with so much to render Lorenzo de' Medici the honour and glory of his age, he manifested no clearer views of religion than those commonly prevalent. He did not, indeed, altogether neglect its outward forms, but he discovered no perception that its essence consists in a renewal of the heart by the Holy Spirit, leading to a saving faith in Jesus Christ; and even at death he displayed much more the equanimity of a pagan philosopher, than the triumphant hopes of a Christian.

CHAPTER II.

Birth and childhood of Giovanni de' Medici, afterwards Leo x.
—Scenery and intercourse in which his youth was passed
— Impiety and licentiousness of Florence — Conspiracy
against Lorenzo's life—Giovanni's natural disposition—His
education—Politian his tutor—Greek refugees in Florence—
Chalcondyles—Lorenzo's opinion of his three sons—Politian's quarrel with their mother—Children removed from
Florence to escape the plague and war—Lorenzo's ambitious
views respecting Giovanni—Methods of attaining them—
Extraordinary preferments of Giovanni—Becomes cardinal
—Rejoicings at Florence—Goes to Rome—Dissolute manners
of Rome—General corruptness of the age.

GIOVANNI DE' MEDICI, afterwards Leo x., was born in Florence, on the 11th day of December, 1475. His elder brother Piero, who came to an untimely and miserable end, was then nearly five years old. Giuliano, the youngest, was not born till 1478. Their education was conducted entirely at home, and Lorenzo doubtless intended that it should be under his own direction; but his avocations were too many to leave him much time for attending to domestic concerns. Whilst he resided at Florence, absorbed in political cares, his family mostly lived at one of his numerous country seats in the neighbourhood of the city. This circumstance was not without its advantages to the youths, as the scenery of the district was well calculated to awaken in their hearts a sympathy with the loveliest forms of nature. No city in Tuscany has a more delightful position than Florence. The Arno, which divides it into two parts, here flows with a noble and somewhat rapid current, through a spacious and verdant vale. The valley is inclosed by hills, clothed with vineyards and olive woods, while the cypress, the pine, and the chesnut, frequently occurring in their most luxuriant growth, impart to the landscape a sombre and stately air. The little valley of Fiesole, in which Lorenzo's nearest rural villa stood, is particularly of enchanting beauty. In the hollow, the torrent Mugnone hastens to unite with the Arno. The hills on either side are terraced with vineyards and groves, villas and gardens. Lorenzo's house was seated between the sloping sides of a mountain, seeming from a distance to be embosomed in woods, but really commanding a full prospect of the whole valley and of the city beyond. The love which Lorenzo had for literature and learned men, brought into this neighbourhood many of the choicest minds which Europe then possessed. The villas in this valley of Fiesole were inhabited by such men as Landino, Scala, Ficino, Pico, and Politian, the revivers of letters as the dark ages of history passed away—a society which has been characterized as "superior perhaps to that of the boasted sages of Greece." To these were added, at various periods, artists of world-wide celebrity—Michel Angelo Buonarotti, the painter and sculptor, and Torregiano, his great adversary; Giuliano de' san Gallo, the architect of some of the finest structures in Italy of that age; with many other illustrious men, who found in the gardens, museums, and libraries of the Medici, abundant means of improving their knowledge, and refining their taste for the several pursuits to which they devoted their lives. But, however intellectual the circle may have been in which Giovanni de' Medici was accustomed to move from his youth, the religion of Christ appears to have received within it a very doubtful homage, and these eminent men scarcely frowned, if indeed they did not smile, on the licentious habits of their age. Even the grave Lorenzo, whose mind was so heavily engrossed with affairs of state, found leisure to write songs for the carnival festivals, the indecencies of which render them wholly unfit for translation; while the passions of jealousy, envy, and revenge, were so fearfully indulged, that it was not at all unusual or unnecessary to wear armour beneath the clothes, to protect life from the dagger of the assassin. Giovanni was not three years old when an assault of this kind was committed, which, had it succeeded, would have left him fatherless, and which strikingly reveals the awful depth of profligacy to which all classes had sunk. Lorenzo had incurred the enmity of pope Sixtus IV. and his nephew Girolamo Riario, who therefore resolved to take away his life, and the nephew of the latter, the young cardinal Riario, undertook the execution of the plot. He accordingly expressed to Lorenzo a desire to attend Divine service at the church of the Reparata, and to gratify his wish Lorenzo invited him and his suite to his house in Florence. His design was to have Lorenzo and his brother Giuliano assassinated in the church at the moment of the elevation of the host. Being unable to secure the services of any soldier to execute the deed in so sacred a place, he engaged two *ecclesiastics*, who had no such scruples. The priests took their stations near their intended victims—the bell rang—the consecrated wafer was raised—the people bowed—and at the same instant the assassins aimed their blows at Lorenzo and his brother. Lorenzo was only wounded in the neck, and in the confusion which ensued escaped without further injury; but his brother fell, stabbed in nineteen different places. This is no rare example of the melancholy state of morals at the close of the fifteenth century. It was hardly possible that, under the influence of such modes of thinking, writing, and acting, the young mind of Giovanni should be imbued with the highest principles of morality. His natural disposition, indeed, may be said to have been in many respects good. He was amiable, not unforgiving, inclined to be generous, but fond of ease and indulgence. He was sedate beyond his years; and if not so athirst for wisdom as his flatterers would represent, yet amidst the cultivated society of Florence, and the extensive collections of curiosities in literature and the arts which his ancestors had brought together, he could not but imbibe a relish for intellectual pursuits. His education was intrusted to one of the most learned men of the time, Politian, who was also Lorenzo's intimate friend. They had studied together in their youth, and now that Lorenzo had succeeded to the power and wealth of his father, Politian aided him with his counsel, sometimes in the perplexities of government, but chiefly in the patronage which he bestowed on literature, science, and the arts. When printing was introduced into Florence in 1471, the first book committed to the press was the works of Virgil, with notes by Politian, and this was followed by many other productions of the Latin classic writers, under his able editorship. At the same period, the study of Greek literature was revived at Florence. The capture of Constantinople by the Turks caused many learned Greeks to seek protection in Italy. Lorenzo had himself studied the language under one of these refugees, the famous Johannes Argyropylus, to whose zeal and ability, as professor in the academy at Florence, it was chiefly owing that the knowledge of the Greek tongue spread so rapidly, not only through Italy, but also in France, Spain, Germany, and England. His successor in the professorship was a native of the same country, Demetrius Chalcondyles, and from him Giovanni and his brothers received their principal instruction in Greek.

Under such singular advantages it was to be expected that the children of Lorenzo would make considerable progress in learning. He is said himself to have expressed the opinion, that his eldest son would be distinguished for ability, his second for probity, and his third by an amiable temper. Politian, in his letters to his friends, often records their proficiency with much self-gratulation. From these letters it would also appear, that there often existed much jealousy and ill-feeling between the tutor and Clarice, the mother of his pupils. She claimed a mother's right to interfere in the instruction of her sons, but to Politian her interference seemed an unpardonable intrusion. " As for Giovanni," he writes, " his mother employs him in reading the Psalter, which I by no means commend. Whilst she abstained from meddling with him it is astonishing how rapidly he improved, insomuch that he read without assistance." From this little incident we may not unfairly conclude, that with the tutor religious instruction was quite a secondary concern. At this time, Giovanni was in his fourth year, and his popularity seems to have commenced already, for Politian writes again, " Giovanni often rides out on horseback, and the people follow him in crowds." Lorenzo could have had but little intercourse with his children during these years, for it was to him the most busy and anxious period of his life. The enmity which Sixtus IV. had discovered in the attempt to assassinate him, was continued through the whole life of the pontiff, and made it necessary for Lorenzo to exert all his powers to baffle the intrigues of his foe. Immediately on recovering from his wound he took measures for self-defence. He endeavoured, not without considerable success, to draw several Italian princes into a league against the pope. In the autumn of 1478, war was declared between the Florentine republic and the papal states, and almost simultaneously Florence was alarmed by the outbreak of the plague, whose direful visitations during the middle ages so often desolated the most populous cities of Europe, and the ravages of which in Florence, on a former occasion, were very extensive. Lorenzo immediately removed his family from both dangers at once, by sending them to Pistoia, a city twenty miles distant, where also he possessed estates. They did not return to Florence till the close of the following year, during the whole of which the plague raged violently, and the war was carried on with various success. Peace was not restored till 1481, when Mahomet II., the captor of Constantinople, meditating still further conquests, descended upon Italy, and seized upon the city of Otranto.

The pope, trembling for the safety of the whole peninsula, instantly made pacific advances to Lorenzo, which were readily accepted, and the Turks were soon expelled by the united arms of the Italians. Peace did not, however, bring with it to Lorenzo leisure and domestic comfort, for now that the state was freed from external assaults, he was anxious to consolidate his power, and improve the various departments of government, in which he so eminently succeeded that it was said, he received his authority brittle as glass, and left it strong as iron.

The death of Sixtus IV., in 1484, delivered Lorenzo from a powerful and malignant foe, and opened a new path to the aggrandizement of his family, which he did not fail to pursue.

At this time, the rich endowments of the papal church were an object of ambition to all the noble families in Europe, and Lorenzo had already determined that Giovanni should seek advancement in this direction. Hitherto, however, the prospect was forbidding, owing to the hostility of the pope. It is true that the candidate for ecclesiastical honours was only nine years old, but in that corrupt age this was no hindrance to church preferment. Indeed, through the favour of Louis XI. of France, he had been the year before appointed abbot of Fonte Dolce, and likewise of the rich monastery of Passignano. At subsequent periods, he had also been made canon of three different cathedrals, rector of six livings, and abbot of thirteen monasteries in various parts of Italy and France, the emoluments as well as the honours of which accrued to the youthful prince, while the duties of all were necessarily delegated to others. Could anything more impressively show the height which corruption had reached in the so-called church, and the imperious necessity for the Reformation, which was then about to commence? Just at this time, the great Reformer, Luther, was born. Thus the course of Giovanni's life (during which the corruptions of the papacy were to reach their greatest height) was decided by the death of Sixtus, in February, 1484, and his renowned antagonist had entered life in the preceding November.

Lorenzo saw that his son's way was now open to the highest offices in the church, and to facilitate his progress took great pains to conciliate the good-will of Sixtus's successor, Innocent VIII. It delighted him to learn that the pope had already expressed a very favourable opinion of him, and he neglected no means of increasing that esteem. Innocent was an old man, and might die before Giovanni could reap the advantage of his friendship. Accordingly, Lorenzo resolved to urge the prompt adoption of measures to that end, and sent his eldest son Piero to Rome, accompanied by his tutor Politian, with instructions to ingratiate himself in every way with the pope for his brother's sake. He also wrote the pontiff earnest letters of intreaty, that Giovanni might be included in the next batch of cardinals. The pope seems to have felt, if not the impropriety, at least the danger of conferring the high dignity on so young a candidate. But, after many anxious months of delay, Lorenzo's ambitious hopes were gratified, and in November, 1488, before Giovanni had completed his thirteenth year, the announcement reached Florence, that he was numbered among the chief dignitaries of Rome, accompanied only with the condition that he should not publicly assume the insignia of his rank for the space of three years. He spent this interval at the academy of Pisa, studying the scholastic theology and ecclesiastical jurisprudence. When at length the day arrived for his public investiture, great preparations were made to celebrate it with splendour, both in the mansion of Lorenzo and in the city of Florence, for the elevation of Giovanni was regarded by the citizens as an honour conferred upon themselves. On Sunday, the 9th of March, 1492, in the monastery of Fiesole, the superior, having first blessed the scarlet mantle and hat, arrayed the youth in the gorgeous vestments peculiar to the cardinals of Rome. The company then retired to a repast, after which the young cardinal was conducted to the city in great state, surrounded by the prelates and chief magistrates, and preceded by his brother Piero, who was mounted on a fiery steed, caparisoned with gold, and followed by an immense multitude, who made the air ring with their shouts and acclamations. Illuminations and fireworks concluded the festivities of the day.

In the same week, the cardinal left Florence for Rome, which was to be his future place of abode. The exchange was certainly not for the better. Hitherto the popes had rather discouraged than patronised the progress of letters. They were by no means anxious that the world should become enlightened. In almost every other city of Italy, the interests of literature and science were attended to with greater assiduity than in the papal metropolis. Here also profligacy and impiety were more prevalent than elsewhere. Superstitious regard for rites and ceremonies characterized the ignorant; atheism, or a pagan kind of deism, the educated class. The former thought to make compensation for their criminal habits by occasional penances and fasts, the latter indulged their sinful propensities without restraint, and secretly laughed at the credulity which imposed such restraint upon others. The cardinal De' Medici was in a dangerous position for any man, how much more for a youth whose heart was unrenewed by the Spirit of God, and who was naturally disposed to ease and indulgence! His stay, however, for the present, was brief; and on the occasion of being presented to the pope and cardinals, he conducted himself with great dignity, and a gravity beyond his years. Yet it makes one shudder to reflect, that of these cardinals who now gave him the kiss of fraternal recognition, the eldest was the notorious Roderigo Borgia, and another that Raffaelle Riario, who had attempted the murder of his father, and accomplished that of his uncle. Among such associates were his future years to be passed; so completely had ambition overpowered, both in Lorenzo and in his son, the considerations of morality, and even the feelings of resentment.

CHAPTER III.

Reverses—Death of Lorenzo—Cardinal's letter to his brother—His worldly and ambitious aims—Returns to Florence—Recalled to Rome by the death of Innocent VIII.—Roderigo Borgia the new pope, as Alexander VI.—His infamous life—Cardinal retires to Florence—Lodovico Sforza of Milan—Charles VIII. invades Italy—His character—Approaches Florence—Savonarola, the Florentine reformer—The Medici quit Florence.

HITHERTO uninterrupted prosperity had attended the course of the youthful De' Medici, but a succession of calamities now awaited him, that should have sufficiently instructed him how vain and unsatisfying is the attainment of our most ambitious earthly hopes. The first of these was the death of his father, which occurred a few weeks after the cardinal's departure for Rome. Lorenzo had been unwell for a considerable time, but early in April, 1492, the disorder assumed a more serious aspect. It baffled the skill of his physicians, and when Lazaro da Ticino, a man of great medical reputation, was summoned to the bedside, he could only conceal his own ignorance of the complaint, by administering medicine containing such unheard-of ingredients as pearls, and jewels mixed with the most expensive potions. The death of Lorenzo took place on the 8th of April, 1492, and when published in Florence it produced throughout the city extraordinary excitement, spreading consternation amongst those who favoured the present order of government. But there were none, however hostile to the De' Medici, who refused a tear to the memory of a man who had done more than all others to enrich and dignify the Florentine republic. The news soon reached Rome, and on the 12th of April we find the cardinal De' Medici writing to his brother Piero in the following terms :—

"The cardinal Giovanni de' Medici, at Rome, to Piero de' Medici, at Florence.

"My dearest brother, now the only support of our family, what I have to communicate to thee, except my tears, I know not ; for when I reflect on the loss we have sustained in the death of our father, I am more inclined to weep than to relate my sorrow. What a father we have lost ! How indulgent to his children ! Wonder not, then, that I grieve, that I lament, that I find no rest. Yet, my brother, I have some consolation in reflecting that I have thee, whom I shall always regard in the place of a father. Do thou command—I shall cheerfully obey. Thy injunctions will give me more pleasure than I can express ; order me—put me to the test—there is nothing that shall prevent my compliance. Allow me, however, my Piero, to express my hopes, that in thy conduct to all, and particularly to those around thee, I may find thee as I could wish—beneficent, liberal, affable, and humane, by which qualities there is nothing but may be obtained—nothing but may be preserved. Think not that I mention this from any doubt that I entertain of thee, but because I esteem it to be my duty. Many things strengthen and console me ; the concourse of people that surround our house with lamentations, the sad and sorrowful appearance of the whole city, the public mourning, and other similar circumstances—these in a great degree alleviate my grief; but that which relieves me more than the rest is, that I have thee, my brother, in whom I place a confidence that no words can describe, etc.—From the city, 12 Ap. 1492."

Although in this letter there is nothing strictly reprehensible, yet it is impossible to avoid noticing the calmness and self-possession which the writer exhibits, under a calamity that naturally calls forth signs of the most poignant grief. It is astonishing, and gives no little insight into the nature of Giovanni de' Medici, that in so short a letter, written on so heart-rending an occasion, he should dwell so particularly on the deportment which would be requisite for the safe preservation of the power bequeathed by Lorenzo to his son. The worldly wisdom and politic ambition which characterized the future pontiff, were already discernible in the boy-cardinal. Apparently under the influence of similar motives, he did not hasten to return home, but continued some time longer at Rome, to mature those relations which a short stay there had enabled him to form. Perfectly aware, as his letter manifests, of his brother Piero's instability of character, he knew that his presence would be necessary at Florence to preserve the authority of his family in the city. But before leaving Rome, he obtained from the pope the appointment of legate of the Tuscan state, thus gaining from official dignity the weight and importance which others derive from years and experience. On returning to Florence, he found Piero already invested with authority as Lorenzo's successor. The cardinal made every exertion to strengthen his brother's hands, and endeavoured, as far as possible, to tread in the steps of his father. He was discreet in his behaviour, conciliatory to all ranks of the people, and especially munificent to artists and men of learning. Those whom Lorenzo had patronised were particularly the objects of his favour; indeed, these included the most eminent men of their day, whose friendship even with princes rather conferred honour than received it.

For a time it seemed as if the discontented and factious among the citizens were as much awed by the new government as they had been by the former, but this political calm was not destined to continue long. The death of Lorenzo was followed, at a short interval, by that of pope Innocent VIII., who expired July 5th, 1492. This was another serious blow to the hopes of the cardinal De' Medici.

Innocent had from the first encouraged and favoured him, and such powerful influence would have greatly advanced his interests at Rome. He immediately returned thither to attend at the funeral obsequies. On the 5th of August, the remains of the pope were carried to the church of St. Peter, followed by five cardinals, of whom De' Medici was one. Next day, the cardinals assembled in conclave for the election of a successor to the pontifical throne. There were two principal candidates, Roderigo Borgia, and Ascanio Sforza, the latter belonging to the ducal family of Milan, and whose connexions and rank gave him great influence in the college. But Roderigo's long experience and skilful dissimulation, together with the wealth he had amassed during his public life, enabled him to mislead even Sforza himself. The latter became, in fact, the most earnest and powerful supporter of Borgia's pretensions. In return for his services he received four mule-loads of silver, and all the other cardinals, excepting five, took bribes for their votes in the same unblushing and disgraceful manner. To the credit of the young De' Medici, he stood in the list of exceptions, supporting the claims of Francesco Piccolomini, afterwards Pius III.

On the 11th of August, Roderigo, the new pontiff, under the name of Alexander VI., made his entrance in state into the church of St. Peter. In his procession to the church he passed under innumerable triumphal arches, on which inscriptions were placed, composed in terms of the grossest flattery, and even blasphemy. One of these pronounced him to be "invincible, most pious and magnificent, and in all things pre-eminent." Another, comparing him with Sixtus his predecessor, concluded with, *Ille vir, iste deus;* " The first was a man, the last is a god."

So deep was the degeneracy of the Roman people, that they could attach such lofty epithets to a name that has become infamous for all time through the transcendent profligacy of its wearers. Neither can the excuse be urged, that the wicked acts of Borgia were committed, or at least discovered, at a later period; for no sooner was the election made public, than a general alarm seized the rulers of the Italian states from their knowledge of his character. Ferdinand of Naples is said to have shed tears, which not even the death of his children could draw from him, prophetically declaring to his queen, that this event would be destructive to the peace of Europe. In private life, Borgia had outraged even the common rules of decency, and his public career had been a continual source of extortion, oppression, and deceit. Rome was no longer a safe place of abode for the cardinals who had opposed the election of the new pope. They fled in various directions; and the cardinal De' Medici returned to Florence, hoping to support by his presence the declining authority of his brother, for Piero had given early evidence of his incapacity to govern, and this revived the hopes of many who still cherished a spirit of hostility to the Medici, and opposed their dominancy in the state. During the life of Lorenzo their enmity had been restrained, if not subdued, by the undoubted success of his measures, and the lustre they reflected on the government. He had also contented himself with exerting influence rather than authority in his native city, and thus had greatly repressed the jealousy excited by his power. His attention had been chiefly directed to securing for Florence the respect of the neighbouring sovereigns, and preserving between the various states of Italy such a balance of power, as should secure peace to the whole. In this he was aided, not less by the central position which Florence occupied among those states, than by his high character and political sagacity.

The far less comprehensive mind of Piero was too much engrossed with plans of aggrandizement at home to give much attention to the common good of Italy; and in the hope of obtaining supreme power within the walls of Florence, he formed a secret league with the king of Naples, and endeavoured to ingratiate himself with the pope. On this being discovered by Lodovico Sforza, at that time guardian of the young duke of Milan, who was his nephew as well as his ward, it excited in him apprehensions lest his own power should be assailed, and his own ambitious aims be thwarted by those of Piero; for, having been the real holder of power during the long minority of the young duke, Lodovico was extremely loath to part with it when he should come of age, and was accordingly busily contriving a plot for supplanting his nephew. As the latter was connected by marriage with the king of Naples, who would naturally resent any injustice done to his relative, Lodovico regarded with more jealousy the union lately formed between Piero and Ferdinand, and to counteract its influence drew into a defensive league with himself both the Venetians and the pope.

Towards the middle of 1493, Lodovico was alarmed to hear that the pope had proved unfaithful to his engagements, by entering into an alliance with Ferdinand of Naples. The chief bond of this compact was a marriage between Ferdinand's grand-daughter, Sancia of Aragon, and Geoffroi Borgia, the youngest son of the pope. Lodovico now saw, that to accomplish his purposes it would be needful to strengthen himself by alliance in some other quarter, and conceived the desperate project of inviting the invasion of Italy by a foreign prince. The monarch to whom he directed his eyes was Charles VIII. of France.

Charles was by no means fitted by nature for so adventurous an enterprise as the conquest of foreign states. He had lost both parents in his youth, and his mind had been left to the meagre cultivation it could gain from the wild romances of the age. Suspicious of his own deficiencies, though not acquainted with them, he was jealous of the meanest rival; and it is even said, that when his child died—a fine boy three years old—Charles was not displeased, because, as he gave tokens of a bold and spirited temper, he might possibly, at a future day, become more popular with the people than himself. Neither had Charles any bodily endowments to compensate for his mental defects. Low in stature, weak and ill-proportioned in frame, he was wholly unfit for the achievements and hardships of war. Yet the pernicious reading which he had indulged had so inflamed his imagination, that he fancied himself equal to the most arduous exploits. Over such a mind Lodovico Sforza's keen intellect and impetuous will found little difficulty in securing the mastery. He represented to Charles, by his agents, the undoubted right of the house of Anjou to the throne of Naples, and the ease with which it might be asserted. For the claim which Charles was thus encouraged to set up there was some, though a slender foundation. Two centuries before, the ancestors of the French king had been expelled from Italy by those of Ferdinand. But both parties, when holding the sceptre, had looked to the pope for a justification of their tenure, and each had, in turn, received the papal benediction, with consent to their keeping the throne. Both had obtained the sovereignty by usurpation and fraud, and received confirmation of it from an arbiter who had neither right nor power to decide. But if the original title of both claimants was equally groundless, the superior right of Ferdinand to the present possession could not be questioned, and there was no fair pretext whatever for the French king's disturbing the peace of Italy for the sake of vindicating his antiquated claims. So powerfully, however, had Lodovico wrought upon Charles's weak mind, that he fancied himself destined not only to the conquest of Italy, but to roll back upon Asia the tide of Turkish invasion, and to recapture the holy sepulchre from the profane hands into which it had fallen. He accordingly made preparations for this new and romantic crusade.

His resources, indeed, were very inadequate to the occasion. "The king," says Comines, "had neither money nor talents for such an enterprise. Before his departure he had to borrow one hundred thousand francs from a banker at Genoa, at an enormous interest, as well as to resort to other plans for assistance. He had neither tent nor pavilion, and in this state he began his march into Lombardy. One thing only seemed favourable to him—he had a gallant company, consisting chiefly of young gentlemen, though with little discipline." It may be safely asserted, that had Lorenzo de' Medici still lived, or his place been filled by any other capable of uniting the various Italian states in a league for self-defence, the expedition of Charles must have utterly failed. His strength consisted, and his success arose, from the divided condition of Italy itself.

While making preparations at home, Charles took the precaution of sounding the various potentates of Italy, to ascertain if he might count on the assistance of any. From Lodovico Sforza he of course received promises of aid. But the pope earnestly dissuaded him from his purpose, and urged him to submit his claims to the papal judicature. This reply so irritated Charles, that he vowed he would expel Alexander from the pontifical throne.

The Florentines felt that their position was a dangerous one, and therefore attempted to conciliate the invader. Guided by the counsel of Piero, they sent word to Charles that they wished well to his undertaking, but begged to be excused discovering their friendship at present, lest they should fall a sacrifice to the resentment of Ferdinand, who might forthwith invade the Tuscan territory. This subterfuge rendered Charles so indignant that he drove the ambassadors from his presence, and ordered the immediate banishment from Lyons of the agents of Piero de' Medici, where the family had for years carried on the business of banking. It was evident that the king suspected Piero to be the cause of the Florentine opposition.

It was in August, 1494, that Charles commenced his march; though troops had been sent forward some months earlier, under the duke of Orleans, between whom and the soldiers of Ferdinand some skirmishes had taken place, in which the latter were repulsed. The French king advanced without interruption till he came within sight of the Apennines at Asti, where Lodovico Sforza met him, accompanied by his duchess, the splendour of whose dress and equipage astonished the French. Charles's stay at Asti was marked by the grossest licentiousness, in consequence of which he felt so ill that his life was endangered. On reaching Milan, the king had an interview with the young duke and duchess. The latter implored his interference on behalf of her husband, who, through the tyranny and usurpation of Lodovico, was then lying at the point of death. Her intreaties and tears made no impression on Charles's depraved heart; and his traitorous ally, Lodovico, was soon after saluted as duke of Milan by the corrupt populace, and still corrupter magistrates, of the city.

Charles was now at the very confines of the Florentine state, and his approach excited the utmost consternation among all who were well affected to the present government. On the other hand, there were many who hoped that this invasion would lead to the expulsion of the De' Medici from power. Foremost among them were two citizens, who were descended from Francesco de' Medici, brother of Cosmo the Great, who, regarding with great jealousy the exclusive tenure of power which the other branch of their family enjoyed, had formed a considerable party to favour the designs of Charles.

But far more influential than these was the celebrated Reformer of Florence, Savonarola. This man appears to have been one of the most earnest of that somewhat numerous class, in whose minds the light feebly glimmered before the dawn of the Reformation. Without possessing just views of the way of salvation—without understanding that a man is justified before God only by faith in Christ—Savonarola saw the monstrous incongruity between a profession of Christianity, and such dissolute habits of life as then prevailed throughout Italy. His political sympathies were also on the popular side, for the people seemed to him led blindfold, as indeed they were, by priests and nobles. During the time of Lorenzo, he had boldly and eloquently denounced from the pulpit of San Marco the oppressive exactions of the great, and the depravity of the citizens in general. When Lorenzo lay at the point of death, he demanded admission to his presence. Standing before the dying man, he exhorted him to repentance, and conjured him, in case of recovery, to lead a virtuous and well-regulated life. The influence of Savonarola with the common people was very great, and the spirit of partisanship often ran so high as to produce battles in the streets. Savonarola seems to have dreaded the ravages which the invading army might be expected to commit, and to have charged Piero de' Medici with being the author of the French king's resentment. Piero found himself deserted by the majority of the inhabitants, and, filled with vexation and alarm for his own safety, resolved on the perilous experiment of throwing himself at the feet of Charles. He hastily left the city, and hastened to Sarzana, a place fortified by Lorenzo, and before which Charles's troops were encamped. On being introduced to the king, Piero behaved with a pusillanimity that rendered him contemptible in the eyes of the French. They heard in astonishment his offers to give up strong fortresses and valuable cities into the hands of the king. Charles treated him with disdain, and Piero dejectedly returned to face the citizens of Florence. But the news of his behaviour had outstripped him, and had so incensed the republicans that they refused him admission. A tumult occurred at the gates, in which Piero narrowly escaped with his life, but succeeded in entering the city. Here the crowds greatly increased, and the enemies of the De' Medici used their utmost efforts to provoke the people against Piero and his brother. Missiles were discharged from the windows and the roofs of the houses, and although the cardinal raised the cry of "Palle! palle!"* so long the watchword of the De' Medici, the charm seemed to be dispelled, and the clamour grew fiercer each moment. The brothers resolved on taking to flight; Piero

* The Palle, or golden balls, were the heraldic arms of the family.

and Giuliano fled to Bologna, and the cardinal, after vainly seeking a refuge in Savonarola's convent of San Marco, at length reluctantly left the city, disguised as a monk, and hastening through the passes of the Apennines, joined his brothers in their retreat.

CHAPTER IV.

Charles VIII. enters Florence—Passes through Rome—Neapolitans make vain resistance — Charles enters Naples in triumph—Italian league against him—Charles crowned at Naples—Slowly retraces his steps—His losses in the battle of the Taro—Disorders at Florence—Influence of Savonarola—Attempts of the Medici to regain authority—Martyrdom of Savonarola—The cardinal determines to travel—Returns and settles in Rome.

THE progress of Charles VIII. to the south seemed more like a triumphal procession than the march of an invading army. He had few obstacles to overcome, and these speedily gave way at his approach. On the expulsion of the Medici from Florence, he directed his steps thither, and, although at first the citizens were greatly alarmed, under the apprehension that he intended to take their city by force, when they found that he was peacefully disposed, they received him with every demonstration of joy. On the 17th of November, he made his public entry into Florence, riding on horseback, under a rich canopy, and guarded by his barons and officers. He was met by a deputation of the chief inhabitants, and conducted to the now forsaken palace of the Medici, which had been prepared for his reception. His visit was celebrated with feasting, illuminations, and public shows, which so much pleased the puerile mind of the French king, that he continued in Florence much longer than prudence would have dictated. During his stay he formed the design of reinstating the Medici in their authority, and sent letters after Piero to recall him. But Piero was already beyond reach, for, meeting at Bologna with no agreeable reception, he had proceeded to Venice, and there, under the advice of the senate, he determined to remain. The very design of restoring him was, however, sufficient to arouse the anger of the Florentines, and tumults ensued, which threatened to terminate in bloodshed. They were at length quelled by the citizens consenting to pay the king one hundred and twenty thousand florins, and by Charles's agreeing to the banishment of the Medici to a distance of one hundred miles from the city. On advancing upon Rome, the invader found a free admission. Indeed, the pope had been so generally deserted by his nobles, that any attempt at opposition must have proved futile. Charles remained in the metropolis for a month, and behaved in all respects as though he were sole master of the city.

In the meantime, some preparations were made by the Neapolitans for disputing his further advance. Ferdinand had suddenly expired early in this year, and his son Alfonso had succeeded him in the throne. But in the few months that intervened, Alfonso had so alienated the affections of his subjects by oppression and cruelty, that he found it impossible to offer any successful resistance to his powerful foe; and when, in January, 1495, he received the news of Charles's entry of Rome, and of the retreat of the Neapolitan troops, he saw that there was no course open to him but to abdicate his crown, and flee for his life. He escaped into Sicily, beyond the reach of the invading conqueror, and left the government, with all its difficulties, in the hands of his son Ferdinand II. This young prince used his utmost exertions to defend the kingdom from the invader, but he had come too late to the throne for any efforts to succeed. His nobles rapidly deserted him, and after a few attempts to check the march of Charles's army, in which he was feebly supported by his subjects, and treacherously abandoned by some of his principal officers, he resolved on leaving his kingdom in the hands of the enemy. He hastened to the harbour, and took ship for the island of Ischia, where he possessed an important fortress. As he receded from the shore, and the edifices of Naples grew dim in the distance, the fugitive king was heard often repeating the words of the psalmist, " Except the Lord keep the city, the watchman waketh but in vain," Psa. cxxvii. 1.

Charles VIII. entered Naples February 22nd, 1495, and was received with public rejoicings. Few features of this renowned invasion are more remarkable than the general dislike which the Italian people discovered to their sovereigns, and the mistrust of their subjects exhibited by the rulers. We are pained at the constant repetition of acts of faithlessness, treachery, and ingratitude, on the one hand—of cruelty and mercenary rapacity on the other. The bands of society were dissolved by universal immorality; the governors and the governed were wholly devoid of mutual confidence; and thus the progress of the foe, which, in happier times, would have been easily withstood, became resistless. Alexander VI. gave vent to his contempt for the expedition by ironically observing, that the "French had overrun Italy with wooden spurs, and conquered it with chalk;" alluding to the practice of the French, who, when riding for amusement, used sharp-pointed sticks for spurs; and when billeting the soldiers, marked with chalk the houses where they were to lodge.

Charles continued at Naples till the following May. His time was passed in absurd and puerile amusements, or still more degrading acts of superstition. He regularly attended mass every morning, and was occasionally treated to some of those spectacles, which the priests of that age palmed off upon the ignorant and superstitious as miracles. On visiting the church of St. Januarius, they exhibited to him the head of the martyr, and produced a vessel containing something congealed at the bottom, which they declared to be the martyr's blood. At their request, Charles touched it with a silver wand, and on being placed upon the altar before the head it forthwith began to melt, grow warm, and boil, to the astonishment of the king and his courtiers, who were assured that this blood was privy to the secrets of Heaven, and never dissolved but at the prayers of the just. His public entertainments were chiefly tournaments, and spectacles of the most expensive and gorgeous description.

But while the French king was thus wasting his time at Naples, his enemies were arousing themselves from their lethargy. The usurping duke of Milan, having attained the object of his ambition, now perceived that his own safety, together with that of all the Italian princes, was endangered by Charles's conquest of Naples. He accordingly persuaded the republic of Venice and the pope to enter into league with himself, to intercept Charles on his return through the northern states to France. Ferdinand of Spain and the emperor Maximilian were also parties to the convention, the aid of the former being solicited by the exiled king of Naples.

When Charles heard of the alliance thus formed against him, he determined on returning quickly, before the allies could have time to mature their plans. Nevertheless, several circumstances contributed so to retard his march and weaken his forces, as to render the retreat extremely perilous, and in the event disastrous. First of all, he would be crowned at Naples in great state, as king of France, Sicily, and Jerusalem. Then he judged it requisite to leave garrisons in the various fortresses of the kingdom, and although his progress to the north was unobstructed, yet he lost so much time in receiving deputations, and making grand entries into the cities that lay in his route, that six weeks elapsed before he gained sight of the Apennines. He passed these barriers, however, without opposition, but on descending into the plains of Lombardy, he perceived the tents and pavilions of the allied army pitched on the banks of the Taro, one of the numerous streams of the Apennines which feed the river Po. Anxious, if possible, to avoid a conflict, which would certainly diminish his strength without giving him any real advantage, even if victorious, Charles demanded permission to pass unmolested to his own dominions, offering at the same time to pay for all necessary supplies of provisions. But the allies were resolved on battle, and both parties prepared for it with great devotional ceremony. "On Monday, the 6th of July," says the garrulous Comines, "the gallant king Charles, in complete armour, mounted his horse 'Savoy,' which was presented to him by the duke of Savoy. He was the finest horse I ever saw; his colour was black, he had only one eye, was of a middle size, but well proportioned to his rider, who seemed on this occasion to be quite a different being from that for which nature had intended him, both in person and countenance, for he always appeared, and is still, timid in his speech, having been educated among low and effeminate people; but on this occasion his horse gave dignity to his appearance; his countenance was firm, his complexion ruddy, and his expressions bold and judicious, insomuch that they reminded me of the promise of Savonarola, that God would lead him by the hand, and that his honour would still be preserved to him." The French made the attack by attempting to cross the river full in the face of the enemy. The undisciplined Italians rushed confusedly on their foes, and the king himself was soon in the midst of the conflict, often being in danger of capture. Both armies were in disorder, and victory would quickly have fallen to the Italians, if they could only have been persuaded to listen to the exhortations of their commanders. But they were too intent on plunder to heed anything besides, and forgetting that the enemy had yet to be conquered, they eagerly seized on the rich spoils which the French had brought with them from Naples, and shared them amongst themselves. As soon as they had gained their object, they dispersed to their own homes. The French claimed the victory, because they had succeeded in passing the stream, but such a victory was worse to them than many a defeat has been. Charles re-entered France, after some other delays, in October, 1495, with the remains of his army, amounting to 5,500 men, about one-fourth of the original number, and these diseased, without clothing or food—a most pitiable exposition of the folly and selfishness which devised and conducted the entire expedition.

The citizens of Florence were now at liberty to choose for themselves some new form of government. Under the influence of Savonarola's preaching, they resolved it should be completely republican. He affirmed that he was Divinely authorized to declare, that the citizens at large were entitled to the legislative power, and that Jesus Christ had engaged to become their king. Two councils were formed, the larger consisting of one thousand citizens, the smaller of eighty of mature age. A medal was struck, having on one side the Florentine device, or *fleur de lys*, with the motto, *Senatus, populus que Florentinus*—"The senate and people of Florence;" and on the other a cross, with the motto, *Jesus Christus Rex noster*—"Jesus Christ our King." That there was fanaticism in such a procedure cannot be denied. Indeed, much of the conduct of Savonarola and his followers bears a strong resemblance to that of our own Fifth Monarchy men, in the times of the Commonwealth.

The government now established was not likely to please those who thirsted for political power, and the contentions and street brawls which so often disturbed the peace of Florence, raged at this time more vehemently than ever. These dissensions within the walls appeared to the banished Medici to furnish a favourable opportunity for regaining their lost ascendency. During the invasion of the French, the cardinal and Giuliano had dwelt chiefly at Rome or Bologna, but Piero had accompanied the victorious army through the greater part of its career.

They now used every exertion to raise funds and equip a sufficient force to re-open to them the gates of their native city. This new army was intrusted to the command of their kinsman, Orsino, who had escaped from the custody of the French king after the battle of the Taro. But Orsino proved unfaithful to his trust, and hearing that the Florentines were prepared to defend themselves, and receiving large offers for his assistance to the French garrison of Naples, who were on the point of being expelled from that city, he marched thither with all his forces, and abandoned altogether the cause of the Medici. Early in 1497, the brothers resolved to renew the attempt. The distractions of Florence continued to increase. The inability of men taken from their stalls and shops to carry on the government of the city became increasingly apparent, and the partisans of the Medici within the walls gave intimation to Piero of their readiness to co-operate with any force that they might send. The pope himself favoured the undertaking, being highly exasperated with Savonarola, for his unflinching exposure of ecclesiastical enormities. The Venetians, also, promised their assistance. Nevertheless, the enterprise failed. Having been delayed by a heavy fall of rain, the Medici learned on approaching the town that the Florentines were apprised of their coming, and had made sufficient preparations for a vigorous defence. After a consultation of four hours, whether they should carry the place by storm, they decided that their forces were not equal to the attempt, and retired in haste to Siena.

The authority of Savonarola had now reached its highest pitch, and the enmity felt against him by his opponents was proportionably strong. Among other methods to counteract his influence, they had procured two Franciscan monks to preach down his doctrines. Savonarola called to his assistance a brother monk, named Domenico da Pescia. In the course of their theological debates, Domenico was so far carried away by his zeal, as to propose to prove the truth of his doctrines by walking through the flames, provided any of his adversaries would consent to the same test. The challenge was accepted by a Franciscan friar, equally inflamed with enthusiasm. The day was appointed, and the place of trial prepared. A heap of fagots was laid in a public street, and over it a platform constructed, so that when the flames blazed up the disputants might walk through them. The whole city gathered together to witness the scene. The flames were kindled, and expectation had risen to its height, when Savonarola interfered, and declared that his friend should not enter the fire without bearing the consecrated wafer in his hand. The proposal shocked the sentiments of the people, who regarded it as sacrilegious and impious. From that moment Savonarola lost his influence; the applause of the populace was exchanged for hootings and curses, and being followed by the mob he was seized, dragged to prison, and finally given over for judgment to an ecclesiastical tribunal appointed by the pope. His fate was of course sealed from that moment. At first, he eloquently vindicated himself from all the charges laid against him; but when the Romish church's most convincing argument—the torture—was employed, his firmness gave way, and he acknowledged that his claims to inspired direction were false. He was instantly carried back to the place that had been prepared for the ordeal, and there, on the 23rd of May, 1498, with two associates, one of whom was the monk Domenico, having been first strangled, his body was burned, after which the ashes were collected and thrown into the Arno.

Hoping that the death of Savonarola had removed the great hindrance to their return to Florence, the brothers De' Medici resolved on making a third effort to accomplish their wishes. By the aid of the Venetians they raised a large body of infantry, and approached the eastern passes of the Apennines. These, however, were already so well guarded by the Florentine troops, that long delays occurred, and it became impossible to find provisions for the army. The Medici secretly sought their own safety in flight, and the soldiers being compelled to lay down their arms, were permitted to return in disgrace to their own country.

The brothers now relinquished for the present all hopes of regaining authority in Florence. Piero entered into the service of the French, and the cardinal determined on improving his knowledge of society by foreign travel. He set out with his cousin Giulio and ten other young men, with whom he was on terms of intimate friendship. They laid aside all the outward decorations of their rank, and agreed, for the sake of amusement, that each should command the party in turn. Passing through Venice, Germany, Switzerland, Flanders, and France, and remaining long enough in each country to acquaint themselves with what was worthiest of note, they returned homewards by sea. The cardinal took up his permanent abode in Rome early in the year 1500, receiving from the pope a much more friendly description of treatment than before. Whether the crafty pontiff dreaded his influence, or wished to conciliate his regard, cannot be determined, but from that time he appeared to lay aside his hostility, and treated the cardinal with attention and respect.

CHAPTER V.

Reckless usurpations of pope Alexander vi.—The pope's family—Extraordinary murder of the duke of Gandia—Cæsar Borgia's profligacy and crimes—His ambition and military exploits—Louis xii. of France employs him—Borgia's treachery and murder of his chief officers—The Medici unite with Borgia—The cardinal retires from public life—His love of ease—Extravagant habits—Death of Alexander vi.—His abandoned character and impiety—Origin of the "Pasquinade"—Reflections on the height to which the profligacy of the age had grown.

ALEXANDER VI. was now firmly seated on the papal throne, and, following in the steps of former pontiffs, but far exceeding them in the boldness of his measures, he zealously sought the aggrandizement of his family. He had four children, Giovanni, Cæsar, Geoffroi, and Lucretia. The eldest son, Giovanni, had been dignified by the Spanish court with the title of duke of Gandia. Cæsar was seeking his fortunes in the church, and had already received a cardinal's hat. Lucretia became about this time the wife of Giovanni Sforza, lord of Pesaro, having been divorced from her first husband. To enrich his eldest son, Alexander resolved on seizing the possessions of the Orsini, a powerful family, who had awakened his jealousy by their too close alliance with the French. The duke of Gandia commanded the expedition, which was intended to perpetrate this act of oppression, and with him was associated the duke of Urbino, a general of established reputation. But the Orsini made so vigorous a resistance, that, after an engagement of some hours' duration, the duke of Urbino was taken prisoner, and with much difficulty the duke of Gandia effected his escape.

This firstborn of the pope shortly after lost his life, under circumstances that develop at once the unnatural cruelty of Cæsar Borgia, his brother, and the general profligacy of that age. The two brothers had been spending an evening at the house of their mother, Vanozza, and, on returning home, the duke excused himself from accompanying Cæsar the whole way, as he had another visit to pay. He then bent his steps to the quarter where the Jews resided, and there disappeared from his attendants, in company with a masked stranger. His absence next day was not much noted at the palace, the pope supposing that he was engaged in some of those nocturnal dissipations, in which all classes indulged without restraint. His continued absence, however, provoked inquiry, and the investigation which followed led to the suspicion of his having been murdered. A boatman of the Tiber declared, that on the preceding night he had seen two persons come down a street which led to the river, and there look carefully about to observe if any person were passing that way. Presently afterwards, a man appeared on a white horse, having behind him a dead body, the head and arms hanging on one side, and the feet on the other. On arriving at the place where filth was commonly discharged into the river, the horse was turned round with his tail towards the water, and the two attendants, taking the dead body, threw it far into the tide. The man on horseback then turned round, and, seeing a mantle floating on the stream, asked what it was that looked black. They replied it was a mantle, and by flinging heavy stones upon it they soon caused it to sink. The boatman further said, that he thought it nothing worthy of remark, for in his time he had seen a hundred dead bodies thrown into the same place, about which no inquiries had been made. On searching the river, the duke's body was found, pierced in several places, and with his money and rich ornaments untouched. As it was evident he had not been murdered for the sake of plunder, the suspicion became general, that, as the duke stood in the way of Cæsar's ambitious views, he had been slain by his brother, and not without the connivance of the pope.

From this time, Cæsar Borgia's career was a continued course of crime and cruelty. Disgusted with ecclesiastical restraints, which he eventually threw off altogether, he sought wealth and power by waging oppressive and unjust wars. As long as he lived in Italy, that country was the theatre of internecine strife. Both treacherous and brave, he was equally dangerous as an ally or as a foe. But these very qualities made him so generally successful, that his aid was often solicited, and even by princes who well knew the risk they ran of being deceived.

Louis XII., being now seated in the throne of Charles VIII., was meditating new designs upon the kingdom of Naples, and had sufficient influence at Rome to secure the co-operation of the pontiff and his warlike son. It was agreed that, as a reward for his assistance of Louis, Cæsar should be permitted to seize, unmolested by the French, on the several states of Romagna, and form them into an independent kingdom. In pursuance of this contract, while Louis commenced operations by invading the duchy of Milan, Cæsar Borgia, with French troops, captured the city of Imola. Two branches of the Sforza family were thus, at the same time, broken down. Caterina, having bravely defended the fortress of Forli against Borgia, was sent prisoner to the castle of St. Angelo at Rome; while Lodovico Sforza, whose unpatriotic compact with Charles VIII. had been the source of so many miseries to his country, was immured by Louis in the castle of Loches, and there, shut up in a dark and lonely chamber, closed, after ten years of misery and solitude, his extraordinary career.

The next places successfully besieged by Cæsar Borgia were Pesaro, Rimini, and Faenza. In the capture of the latter city, he was guilty of an act of treachery, which of itself should consign his name to perpetual infamy, though by no means so prodigious in baseness as many of his deeds. This city made a strenuous resistance, and only capitulated at last on condition, among other terms, that its young sovereign, Manfredi, should receive a distinguished appointment under Borgia's command. No sooner, however, was the youthful prince in the tyrant's power, than he sent both him and his brother to Rome, with directions to put them to death, which was accordingly done. Piombino and the state of Urbino soon afterwards fell before the cupidity and reckless ambition of this priestly warrior. Having also conquered the states of Camerino, he gave fresh evidence of his faithless disregard of treaties, and of promises however sacred; for, persuading the lord of that territory, under pretext of treaty, to put himself into his hands, he instantly caused him and his two sons to be cruelly murdered.

But the crowning act of treachery which disgraced this monster's life was, doubtless, that which occurred at Sinigaglia. The story given is this:—Amongst the commanders enlisted in the service of Borgia, were four who belonged to families of the highest rank in Italy. These were Paolo Orsino, Vitellozzo Vitelli, Oliveretto da Fermo, and the duke of Gravina. Alarmed at the success of their own arms, because of the power it lent to Borgia, and fearful lest he should behave as cruelly and treacherously to his servants as he had done to his foes, they resolved on forming a league, which should watch his movements, and check his vaulting ambition. But they did not ,yet understand the deep dissimulation of the man whom they hoped to control. Cæsar pretended that his conquests had all been undertaken for the public good, and promised that if they would yield him the title of sovereign of Romagna, the real sovereignty should rest with themselves. Deceived by his fair professions, they once more consented to serve him, and immediately deliberated on what new district should be invaded by their united force. The city of Sinigaglia was selected, and was speedily compelled to open its gates. Borgia was absent, and the fortress of the city still made some show of resistance, the governor protesting that he would not capitulate except to Borgia himself. Orsino and his colleagues in command sent, therefore, to Borgia, requesting that he would come quickly. He, who knew not how to forgive, saw that this was a good opportunity for revenging himself upon the nobles who had presumed, for a time, to forsake his standard. He marched with his whole army into the neighbourhood of Fano, and there leaving it, proceeded with one hundred horse to the gate of Sinigaglia. On the way he communicated his design to some confidential officers. He told them that when Orsino, Oliveretto, and the others, should advance from the city to meet him, eight of them were to divide themselves into pairs, each pair to single out their man, to occupy his attention till they reached the city, and then to commit him into safe custody in the apartments prepared for the duke. All things happened according to his expectations. The four commanders came out to pay their respects to him, and being conducted back in the way described, these unsuspecting victims were then made prisoners. Vitelli and Oliveretto were immediately strangled, and after a few days Orsino and the duke of Gravina were consigned to the same fate.

It by no means redounds to the credit of the Medici, that they should ever have consented to an alliance with a man so infamously base as Cæsar Borgia. The voice of ambition, however, silenced the whispers of conscience, and the repeated victories of Borgia seemed to point him out as more likely than any other to reinstate them in their lost dignities and power. They accordingly represented to him the advantages which he would derive by marching his troops into the Florentine territory, and effecting a change in the government. Cæsar pretended to assent to the scheme they proposed, and even promised to support Piero's claim to the supreme authority in the city; but in reality he was devising a plan for improving his own interest. Descending with an army of about eight thousand men into the district of Mugello, he sent envoys to Florence, announcing to the citizens on what terms he would withdraw from their neighbourhood. Amongst these conditions, the restoration of Piero de' Medici to his former honours was one. No sooner were the terms made known than the wrath of the people swelled beyond all bounds. But whilst the negotiation was pending, a message came from the pope, peremptorily forbidding his son to take any further steps in the business. Cæsar, however, secured for himself the payment of a large sum of money, but the cause of the Medici was completely abandoned.

These repeated efforts at regaining the government of Florence are not, perhaps, to be attributed so much to the cardinal as to his brothers, especially Piero, by whom the loss was more severely felt, and against whom the hatred of the Florentines was particularly directed. The cardinal was too fond of luxurious repose to interfere very actively in these ambitious and somewhat hazardous undertakings. Indeed, during the latter years of Alexander's pontificate, he had retired into the seclusion of private life, passing his time partly in amusements, and partly in pleasant intercourse with men of letters, or in indulging his passion for the fine arts—a passion which he appears to have inherited from Lorenzo to such a degree, that in all questions of taste he was regarded as a decisive authority. He took great delight also in music, and his palace, we are told, " re-echoed more frequently with the sprightly harmony of concerts, than with the solemn sounds of devotion." His exercises were often of a violent character, and to reduce the corpulence of his frame he especially indulged in hunting, of which he was always inordinately fond.

But, although less active, he was not less ambitious than his brother, or less desirous of regaining the ancient honours of his house. His revenues had been largely drained by the equipment of the expeditions against his native city, and as his habits were of the most expensive kind, in a superlatively luxurious age, he found his resources exceedingly crippled, and quite inadequate to his support. Unwilling to relinquish his custom of giving splendid entertainments, it not unfrequently happened that he was compelled to pledge the silver utensils of his establishment to pay for the feast. When his friends ventured to remonstrate against this ill-timed profusion, he was accustomed to reply, that great men were the work of Providence, and that nothing would be wanting to them if they were not wanting to themselves. Whatever of truth there may be in the sentiment, it was, in this instance, sadly misapplied; for no presentiment of future greatness, however strong, can justify improvidence and excess.

But the time had now arrived for the sudden overthrow of that edifice of power which the Borgias had so ceaselessly toiled to construct. The event which occasioned it was the mysterious death of Alexander VI., which occurred on the 18th of August, 1503. It has been asserted, that both the pontiff and his son inadvertently drank at a banquet some wine which they had caused to be mixed with poison for the destruction of their enemy, the cardinal

Di Corneto, who was a guest at the feast. Certain it is, that at the time of the pope's death Cæsar Borgia was dangerously ill, and there is nothing in the history of those times, or in the character of the men, to discountenance the entire report.

The reign of Alexander VI. abundantly justified the wisdom of Ferdinand's prediction, that his elevation to power would be the ruin of the peace of Europe. His career was, throughout, one of selfish aggrandizement at every risk, and at the sacrifice of every principle of virtue. It would be difficult to decide whether his private or his public life was the more disgraceful, though the former injured comparatively few, while the latter was fraught with mischief to Italy and to mankind.

That he had no respect for the religious creed of which, as pope, he was the nominal guardian, is demonstrated by the fact, that he caused the beautiful Julia Farnese to be painted in the character of the virgin Mary, with himself as supreme pontiff doing homage at her feet. Indeed, the people of Rome, at that period, hardly seemed to expect that a pope should be a model of anything but irreligion and vice. To speak the truth, however, respecting the state of morals, was become dangerous; and hence it was in this age that the Roman pasquinades originated, which are still so prevalent in times of excitement. One of the earliest relates to this pope, beginning

"Vendit Alexander claves, altaria, Christum;"

and may, almost literally, be translated as follows :—

> "Pope Alexander sells the keys, the altar, and his Lord;
> But what of that? shall he who *bought* from selling be debarred?
> From sin to sin he scampers on, from the flame into the fire;
> His country under foreign hoofs he laughs to see expire:
> Tarquin the Sixth, Nero the Sixth, the Sixth is also he,
> Rome's ruin always by the Sixth surely the fates decree."

The historian Guicciardini, who was not likely to overstate the truth, says respecting him, " He united a singular degree of prudence and sagacity, a sound understanding, a wonderful power of persuasion, and an incredible perseverance, vigilance, and dexterity, in whatever he undertook. But in his manners he was most shameless, wholly devoid of sincerity, decency, and truth ; without fidelity; without religion ; in avarice immoderate ; in ambition insatiable ; in cruelty more than barbarous."

Such is the portraiture, drawn by no Protestant hand, of this sovereign of the Romish church. And if he who presided over the then professed religion of Christendom, and claimed to hold in his hands the keys of heaven, was himself so base, it is not to be wondered at if those were corrupt, profligate, and irreligious, who regarded him as Christ's vicar upon earth, and followed him implicitly as their spiritual guide.

CHAPTER VI.

Louis XII. aims at Italian conquests—Divides Naples with Ferdinand of Spain—Disputes arising out of this—Gonsalvo, the "Great Captain"—Battle of Garigliano—Death of Piero de' Medici—Pius III.—Julius II.—Efforts to enlarge the domain of the church—Cæsar Borgia expelled from Italy—League of Cambray—Victories of the French—Warlike exploits of Julius—Lays an interdict on Austria and France—Cardinal de' Medici leads the papal troops—Battle of Ravenna—Cardinal made prisoner—Carried to Milan—Escapes—Julius opens the gates of Florence to the Medici—Death of Julius II.—His character.

THE commotions which the invasion of Charles VIII. produced in Italy were not very speedily allayed. His successor, Louis XII., had the same ambitious designs on the kingdom of Naples, and prosecuted them with greater success. He had entered into a nefarious arrangement with Ferdinand of Spain, by which the Neapolitan territory should be equally divided between them, to the entire exclusion of the reigning family. The plan succeeded. Federigo, the king, at first took refuge with his family on the barren rock of Ischia, but soon afterwards, presenting himself at the French court as a suppliant, Louis made him duke of Anjou, with a pension of thirty thousand ducats, on condition of his relinquishing all pretensions to the Neapolitan crown. But the royal nobles found it more easy to seize than to divide their prey, and a long course of hostilities was the result, between the Spanish and French forces stationed in the south of Italy. The bravery and military skill of the Spanish general, Gonsalvo de Cardona, styled, both by his countrymen and his adversaries, the Great Captain, at length decided the dispute. The French troops retired to the duchy of Milan, leaving Gonsalvo in full possession of Naples and all its dependencies. From that remote period the crown of Naples continued in the Spanish house, till the war of the French revolution overturned this among other European dynasties.

The decisive battle in which the expulsion of the French was completed by Gonsalvo deserves particular mention, because it witnessed the death of Piero de' Medici, the eldest of Lorenzo's family. This battle took place at the river Garigliano, on the 28th of December, 1503. Piero had engaged himself in the French service, and the fortune of the day being adverse to his party, they were crossing the river in retreat, closely pressed by the Spanish cavalry. Piero embarked in a boat with several other persons of rank, taking in charge some heavy pieces of artillery. The boat proved to be overloaded, and foundered, the whole party perishing in the stream. Thus calamitously ended Piero de' Medici's life of adversity, by which, however, it does not appear that he had been effectually taught wisdom, for ambition mingled with imprudence characterized him to the last.

Alexander VI. was succeeded in the papal chair by Pius III., but his reign had scarcely lasted a month, when he was suddenly carried off, as some think, by poison; though it may have been from the exhausting effects of an abscess, under which he had long suffered. His successor was the cardinal Della Rovere, nephew of Sixtus IV., who assumed the tiara under the title of Julius II.

This pontiff is not less notorious for his bold ambition, than Alexander for his profligacy. Alexander had sought the aggrandizement of his family—Julius aimed at that of the popedom; Alexander hoped to establish the Borgias among the royal houses of Italy—Julius thirsted to make all Italy subject to the temporal sway of the pope. He resolved, from the first, to regain to the papal authority all that had been wrested from it by powerful foreign kings, or by turbulent nobles at home. To accomplish this he shrank from no project because it was daring, and was unabashed before any opposition, however strong or determined. It was well for the cardinal De' Medici's temporal prospects, that he had carefully conciliated the regard of the new pontiff, who would have proved an implacable and fierce enemy, but who always did much to advance the interests of his friends, and frequently employed the cardinal in offices of importance and trust.

The first precaution of the new government

was to seize on the person of Cæsar Borgia, whom Julius compelled to renounce the sovereignty of the cities he had conquered in Romagna. Borgia was then banished for life, and after two years of captivity in a Spanish dungeon, from which he escaped by stealth, he fled to his brother-in-law, the king of Navarre, and entering into his service lost his life some years later, being struck by a ball while fighting under the walls of Viana.

In pursuing his intentions of extending the papal territory, Julius received a serious check from the powerful republic of Venice, which held possessions in Romagna, and was by no means willing to retire before the aggressions of the pope. Venice was, at that time, in her highest state of prosperity. Besides engrossing most of the commerce of Europe, her navy and army rendered her formidable to the strongest foe. Ambitious as she was wealthy, she excited by her rapid growth not only the envy, but the jealousy and fear of surrounding states. When Maximilian of Austria demanded a free passage to the south through her territory, she peremptorily refused him, and even marched some troops into the Tyrol, to prove that she had both the ability and the will to resist. Louis XII. was also annoyed by the restraints which she imposed upon his exercise of power in the duchy of Milan. The Spanish king felt aggrieved that she should continue to hold maritime forts in the kingdom of Naples. And, finally, the pope earnestly desired to eject her garrisons from the Romagnese fortresses and cities. It was this general feeling of jealousy and mistrust that led to the celebrated League of Cambray, which eventually effected the dismemberment of the Venetian state, and its partition between the four sovereigns just named.

In pursuance of the articles of this League, the French army, under the renowned Gaston de Foix, entered Lombardy, and drove back the Venetian force, commanded by the impetuous D'Alviano, from town to town, until nothing was left to the republic but its sea-girt capital, which was happily beyond reach of invasion. An incident occurred in the progress of this war strikingly revealing the spirit of the age. After the battle of Chidradadda, in which the French were victorious, Louis determined immediately to express his gratitude by the erection of a church on the field of conflict. Whilst the ground was yet red and wet with the blood of the slain—men slain in defending their country from unjust and ruthless spoilers—the foundations of the church were laid. The edifice was devoted to "Saint Mary of Victory," although, as Roscoe truly observes, "it might with much more propriety have been dedicated to the deities of treachery, of rapine, and of slaughter." So strangely was superstition (for it deserves no better name) united with fierce ambition and the lust of dominion.

While the French were fully occupying the

attention of Venice in the districts more immediately her own, the pope succeeded in planting his authority in the cities of Romagna, from which the Venetian garrisons had been withdrawn. But no sooner had he gained this much coveted prize, than he saw that the whole object of his joining the League of Cambray was accomplished, and he felt but little scruple at forthwith breaking the engagements he had formed. Anxious now to secure his ill-gotten possessions, and fearful that the conquests of the French would give them too predominant a share of power in Italy, he determined to oppose their further progress, and to prop by his support the falling republic of Venice.

The arrogant Julius often waged war with both carnal and spiritual weapons at once. He accordingly laid under interdict the kingdoms of Austria and France and the duchy of Ferrara, until they should abandon hostilities against Venice. The power of the pope to shut as well as to open the gates of heaven had never been questioned. An interdict was supposed to close those gates against all who lay under its ban. In fact, it prohibited all ecclesiastics from performing the rites of their religion, which were thought indispensable to salvation. Children were unbaptized; marriages ceased to be solemnized; men died without the administration of the eucharist or of the last unction; the dead were often unburied, or interred without any blessing from the church. An interdict upon any kingdom was the certain means, therefore, of producing complaints and revolts against the sovereign who had provoked the displeasure of the pope, and kings were always anxious to avoid so serious an evil. On this occasion, Louis XII. sent an ambassador to the pontiff to plead for its removal, but, instead of listening to his remonstrances, the haughty Julius shut the ambassador up in the castle of St. Angelo. The next step of this warlike priest was to head his troops in person, and, laying siege to the city of Mirandula in the midst of a severe winter, when snow was on the ground, and storms filled the air, he fearlessly exposed himself to all the hazards and hardships of a military life. Although Mirandula soon capitulated, Julius was too impetuous to wait patiently for the opening of the gates. Mounting a scaling-ladder, he entered the city, sword in hand, through a breach in the wall. He then hastened to Bologna, but was compelled to retreat by the concurrent approach of the French and a revolt of the inhabitants. The latter testified their joy at the tyrannical pontiff's disappointment, by hurling from its pedestal a brazen statue, which had formerly been erected in his honour, and which ornamented the centre of the city. This figure, which was one of the master-pieces of Michel Angelo, was battered and mutilated, and then dragged in triumph through the streets. It was afterwards re-cast into a cannon, by order of the duke of Ferrara, and ironically dignified with the name of " Julio."

The following year, 1512, the pope and the Venetians called in the assistance of Ferdinand of Aragon, to expel the French from Italy. The declining health of Julius prevented his taking the field in person, as he would otherwise doubtless have done, and the papal troops were, therefore, led this time by the cardinal De' Medici, who acted in conjunction with the Spanish general, Cardona. Bologna again became the first object of attack, but the siege was presently raised by the speedy and effectual aid of the French, under Gaston de Foix. The decisive conflict between the inhabitants of Italy and their foreign invaders was destined to take place under the walls of Ravenna. In April, 1512, Gaston de Foix, anxious to bring the war to an early issue, approached, and laid siege to this city. The cardinal De' Medici was desirous of prolonging the contest, well knowing that the difficulty of finding supplies in a foreign land would be more harassing to the French army, than any direct opposition by force of arms. But Ravenna was garrisoned by friends too important to be left at the mercy of a conqueror, and when De Foix had succeeded in battering down part of the wall, and was about to enter the city, he found himself attacked in the rear, by the combined forces of the Italian and Spanish commanders. A severe cannonading was carried on upon both sides for two hours, without any decided advantage to either. But the duke of Ferrara, changing the positions of his artillery, charged the Italians in their entrenchments with so much fury, as to throw them into fatal confusion. The valour of the Spanish infantry several times renewed the fight, but at length, after one of the bloodiest conflicts of the whole war, the French were victorious, leaving about twenty thousand of both armies dead upon the field. The cardinal De' Medici was made prisoner, with many other illustrious men; while, on the other hand, the young conqueror, Gaston de Foix, was slain by a shot from a harquebus, in the flower of his age and his renown. Indeed, the loss of the French was larger than that of their foes, and in every respect more severe. After plundering Ravenna, cruelly putting the inhabitants to the sword, without distinction of age or sex, and even violating the sanctuary of monasteries in their thirst for blood and booty, the French army returned to Milan, to recover, if possible, by repose, the energy and discipline which it had lost in this sanguinary war.

The cardinal De' Medici accompanied the French as a prisoner to Milan, and was allowed to reside there with the cardinal Sanseverino, who had also been conspicuous in the battle of Ravenna on the side of the French, being clothed in armour, and "looking," says the chronicler, "like another St. George." At Milan, the cardinal De' Medici met with a company of cardinals and prelates, who, in hostility to the pope, had constituted themselves with all due formality into a general council of the church. This council had for some time been annoying the pontiff, and, indeed, if the French arms had proved triumphant in Italy, it might, perhaps, have effected nothing less than his deposition. But in the very precarious, if not declining state of the French authority, it was become simply an object of ridicule to the populace, who amused themselves by derisively saluting the cardinal Carvajal, as he passed along the streets, with the title of *Papa*, because it was supposed that he aimed at securing the pontifical chair for himself. The cardinal De' Medici thought that he might possibly turn this state of things to his own and the pope's advantage. Therefore, secretly obtaining from Julius a plenary power of absolving all who had fought against the church, he was speedily surrounded by crowds, who, notwithstanding they were still rebellious against papal authority, and gave no promises of amendment, nevertheless received full pardon of their crime from the hands of the cardinal legate. To such strange absurdities did superstition conduct the ignorant, and hypocritical priestcraft the wisest, of that degenerate age.

On the same occasion that the cardinal De' Medici had obtained this absolving power from the pope, he had contrived also to despatch to him secret messages, which fully informed him of the distracted state of the French army. Julius now sought the aid of Maximilian of

Austria, and, by large bribes, induced him to withdraw from the French king some Tyrolese troops, which had been largely instrumental in securing the late victory at Ravenna. No fewer than eighteen thousand of these mercenary but brave soldiers now enlisted themselves under the banner of the pope, a step which quickly decided the fortune of the war. Marching rapidly upon Milan, the papal army found that city already forsaken by the French, and cruelly revenged itself for the defeat at Ravenna by slaughtering all of the French name, whether merchants or invalid soldiers, whom they discovered in places of concealment.

When the army of Louis hurried out of Milan, the officers did not forget to carry with them the cardinal De' Medici. But that sagacious man perceived that the confusion of his captors afforded him advantages for escaping which were not likely soon to recur, and, therefore, made the best use of the opportunity. On arriving at the banks of the Po, he pretended to be ill, and obtained permission to spend the night at the rectory of Cairo. He here procured an interview with some persons of rank, who were willing to favour his purpose. Next day, when the passage of the river was to be effected, the cardinal, riding on a mule, lingered till he was among the last who were to cross. Then suddenly a tumult was raised, he was encircled by his friends, and speedily escaped without bloodshed from the hands of the French.

He hastened to Mantua, and there, in the villa of his friend the marquis Gonzaga, found repose from his warlike adventures and fatigues.

Now that the French were wholly expelled from Italy, the pope was at liberty to take measures for its domestic tranquillity, and for the re-establishment of his own influence. The services which the cardinal De' Medici and his brother Giuliano had rendered during the war were fully recognised by Julius, and he resolved, by way of recompense, to reinstate them in their former dignities in Florence. He therefore pretended that, as the Florentines had been rather favourable than otherwise to the French invasion, there could be no safety for the peace of Italy unless the present government were deposed and another established, in which the Medici should have at least a share. The Florentines, however, were unwilling to consent to any such proposals, and made preparations for resistance. The papal troops, under Cardona, the Spanish general, who was accompanied by the cardinal De' Medici as legate of Tuscany, first besieged and captured Prato, a town ten miles from Florence. The Spaniards were furious in the sack of the town, and put to death multitudes of unoffending citizens. There was no check to their violence and cruelty until the cardinal and his brother interfered, at the risk of their own lives, and succeeded in restoring order. These events so intimidated the Florentines, that they consented to receive Giuliano de' Medici as their gonfaloniere, or chief magistrate, who, accordingly, on the last day of August, 1512, re-entered the city from which he and his brothers had been expelled eighteen years before. The cardinal soon followed his brother, to assist him in settling the order of government. He took care, also, that the citizens should be amused with the festivities and public shows for which Florence had been famous in the days of Lorenzo, but which had been either wholly suspended or greatly reduced for several years past. It is much to be deplored that, with these exciting pleasures, the immoralities which had degraded the Florentines in former times were also renewed.

But there were patriots in Florence who greatly lamented the return of the Medici, believing that it would lead to the utter extinction of that free spirit which had ever distinguished their city. These formed a secret conspiracy for the assassination of the hated brothers. An accident, however, or rather an interposition of Providence, defeated their design. One of the conspirators negligently dropped from his bosom a paper, containing a list of all the citizens whom they expected to favour their cause. This paper was brought to the magistrates, and discovered to them and to the Medici the animosity that was privately cherished towards them by some of the principal inhabitants of the city.

In the midst of the tumult occasioned by this discovery, news came to Florence, which obliged the immediate departure of the cardinal

De' Medici for Rome. This important intelligence announced the death of pope Julius II., who had expired on the 21st of February, 1513.

This pontiff had swayed the sceptre of the Romish church for ten years, and with a vigour and resolution which, however well suited to a temporal monarch in times of social discord, had considerably tended to undermine the spiritual authority of the popedom. His public acts were not only dictated by insatiable ambition, but too frequently marked by almost savage barbarity. The Venetians said of him, that he was better fitted to be a public executioner than a pope. He is said also to have been addicted to excessive drinking, and many proofs are extant of his possessing that passionate temper which a large use of wine is apt to produce. When Ariosto, the poet, was sent by the duke of Ferrara with a submissive and pacific message, the fierce pontiff ordered him instantly to quit his presence, threatening else to throw him into the sea. When he had expelled the French from Italy, he resolved that the Spanish prince should not long occupy the throne of Naples. "If Heaven be willing," said he, shaking the staff which supported his aged steps, and trembling with rage, " the Neapolitans shall, in a short time, have another master." He died with similar exclamations on his lips: " Out of Italy, ye French! Out, Alfonso of Este!" Through his whole career he was impetuous, overbearing, resolute, and ambitious. These traits of character are admirably expressed in the portrait of Julius II., painted by Raffaelle, which is exhibited in the National Gallery of London. It ought not to be omitted, as a somewhat redeeming feature in his history, that Julius fostered the arts, though he despised literature; and he patronised such men as Bramante the architect, Raffaelle the painter, and Michel Angelo the painter and sculptor. It was during his pontificate that many of the finest Roman edifices, including the cathedral of St. Peter's, were commenced.

The Christian observes with delight how, amidst those scenes of tumult and carnage which disfigure the annals of this period, the hand of Infinite Wisdom was conducting all events to one result. It was the corrupt character of the pope and dignified clergy that prepared the people to receive with favour the doctrines of Luther and Melancthon. What Alexander VI. began, Julius II. carried forward. Where the profligate licentiousness of the former had failed to inspire disgust, the shameless lust of power and reckless cruelty of the latter inflamed with hate. All classes were now ready for some great change. Corruption had reached its limits. The darkness had deepened to blackest night, when the morning star of the Reformation dawned.

CHAPTER VII.

Cardinal De' Medici elected pope—Assumes the title of Leo x.—Coronation—Resolves to establish peace in Europe—His influence on Henry VIII. of England—Louis declares war against Milan, and Henry against Louis—Battle of Novara—Battle of the Spurs—Battle of Flodden Field—Leo succeeds in obtaining peace—State of literature in Italy—Leo encourages the study of Greek—Lascar—Musurus—Leo purchases and prints the works of classic writers—Seeks the aggrandizement of his family—Advises Louis to invade Italy—Florence under the Medici.

THE character of the ruler who should, at such a crisis, succeed to the papal chair, was a subject of profound importance to the destinies of Europe and of the Christian church. There is little reason, however, to suppose that this occupied, to any large extent, the thoughts of the cardinals when they met in conclave early in March, 1513, for the election of a new pope. Each of them was eager to forward either his own claims, or those of some friend who had a better prospect of success. Neither had the cardinal De' Medici been negligent in preparing for this eventful occasion. He had previously secured several members of the college to his interests, and during the week that the deliberations continued, he managed to attach to his cause the influential Rafaello Riario, nephew of Sixtus IV. This probably decided the result, for when the votes were at length delivered for examination into Medici's hands, as chief cardinal deacon, he discovered neither astonishment nor indecorous joy at finding that a majority had been given for himself. The cardinals immediately fell down at his feet to render homage, and he, in return, raised and embraced them. When asked what title he chose to assume, he replied that he would take the name of LEO THE TENTH, a choice probably decided by the prosperity and reputation of those pontiffs who had already borne the name of Leo. One of the windows of the conclave being then broken down, the election was announced to the assembled crowds, whose acclamations soon proclaimed it through the city.

The coronation of pope Leo took place on the nineteenth day of the same month, and on the eleventh of April he went in procession to take formal possession of the Lateran. In accordance both with the practice of the times, and with the taste of the pontiff, these ceremonies were conducted on a scale of extravagant magnificence and splendour. Leo always loved the pomp of public ceremonials, and was not ill-qualified to act in them a conspicuous and dignified part. He was now in the prime of life, not having yet completed his thirty-eighth year. He was tall in stature, and while his limbs were slender his body was corpulent. Altogether, his frame was well formed to display to advantage the gorgeous and flowing drapery worn by monarchs on public occasions. His step was stately, and his manners dignified, yet courteous. His complexion was florid, his features large and striking. To detract from these advantages, his sight was very weak, and his countenance betrayed the absence of a vigorous and resolute will. But even these defects were much relieved by the deliberate cautiousness with which he always acted, and the extreme politeness and gentleness of his demeanour.

On the day appointed for his coronation, he was attired in the habit of a priest, and conducted to St. Peter's by a train of cardinals, and other ecclesiastics of the highest rank. At the great altar, an officer of the cathedral, clothed in the robes of his office, knelt reverently before the pope, and, holding in his hand a bunch of tow, set fire to it, repeating while it burned the admonitory words, *Pater sancte, sic transit gloria mundi;* "Holy Father, thus vanishes the glory of the world." The triple crown was then placed upon his head by one of the cardinals, and the pope concluded the ceremony by solemnly pronouncing his benediction on all present.

But the procession on the 11th of April was a much more splendid affair. This day was the anniversary of the battle of Ravenna, in which Leo had been taken prisoner; and that this circumstance might not be forgotten by the spectators, he rode upon the noble white charger which had borne him upon that occasion. Mounted on this steed, and surrounded by cardinals, prelates, princes, and dukes, from most parts of Italy, and even Europe, he passed slowly through the streets of Rome, delighted with the proofs of his popularity, which saluted him at every step. Around him, and vieing in doing him honour, were powerful priests, who had been the worst enemies of his predecessor ; in his train were nobles, whose fierce feuds had for many years distracted the city and the state, but who were now united in bonds of perpetual amity. Foremost among these were the renowned Orsini and Colonna, between whose families strife had existed for centuries. The houses were covered to the roofs with spectators, whose shouts of " *Palle, Palle, Leone, Leone,*" rent the air. From the windows rich pieces of tapestry waved like banners, on which were emblazoned the arms of the Medici, and other appropriate devices. Beneath his feet were flowers, thickly strewn, and breathing the odours of spring ; and over his head, at intervals, were many triumphal arches, inscribed with mottoes, which spoke the sanguine hopes of the citizens, that Leo's accession was the introduction of a golden age. On reaching the church of the Lateran, he was led to a marble chair beneath the portico, and having taken his seat, was then gently raised from it by three cardinals, to indicate the elevation to which he was now lifted. The nobles were, in the next place, admitted to kiss his feet ; the prelates, more favoured, his hands. Gold and silver medals, commemorative of the event, were then distributed to the cardinals and bishops; and after reposing awhile, the pope returned, in similar state, to his abode in the Vatican.

The change in the papal sovereignty soon produced an evident alteration in the condition of Europe. That forbearance of other powers towards Italy, which the ambition of Julius had not been able to compel, though backed by force of arms, the quieter ambition of Leo secured by politic and sagacious counsels. He was well aware that Louis XII. meditated another descent on the duchy of Milan, and resolved to use every effort to avert a catastrophe, which would pour down a flood of evils on the states of Italy. He, first of all, despatched a letter to the French king, earnestly intreating him to refrain from the threatened invasion. Not expecting, however, that this alone would be effectual, he then endeavoured to unite the monarchs of Europe into a defensive league, especially for the protection of the states belonging to the church. At this time, Henry VIII. sat upon the throne of England, but not having yet reached his twenty-third year. He was full of martial spirit, and burned to emulate the renown which his ancestors had gained by their warlike exploits. He thirsted also for a war with France, in which country the English kings had long claimed possessions. On the mind of Henry the pontiff's representations of the ill consequences certain to result from a French invasion of Italy soon produced the desired effect. Henry first sent a warning to Louis to desist from further warfare with the "Father of all Christians;" and this not proving successful, he despatched a second herald, to demand restitution of Normandy and the other provinces that anciently appertained to the British crown, and in case of refusal to declare war. As the French monarch, of course, resisted the demand, hostilities were quickly commenced; and shortly after Louis had sent into Italy an army of sixteen thousand men to lay siege to Milan, the English king entered France with fourteen thousand soldiers, having also large promises of assistance from Maximilian, emperor of Austria, whom the pope had persuaded to join in the league. Maximilian, however, found it easier to make promises than to perform them. He came with a handful of followers to the English camp, and there offered his personal services to the young island king, at the rate of one hundred crowns a day. Henry willingly overlooked the emperor's breach of contract, feeling highly flattered that the first prince in Europe, and the successor of the Cæsars, should consent to be in even nominal subjection to his authority.

Both in France and in Italy the French flag was dishonoured by this campaign. In Italy, the Swiss forces, still kept in pay by the pope and the duke of Milan, gave battle to the invading army, and utterly routed it, with great slaughter, at Novara, on the 15th of June,

1513. About the same time, the army under Henry, greatly increased by Swiss auxiliaries, encountered the French at Guinegate in Picardy, and put them to flight. So quickly was the event of the day decided, that scarcely a blow was struck; for, on the command to charge being given, the French were seized with an unaccountable panic, and fled in all directions, being followed at full gallop by the enemy: from which strange occurrence this battle has been ludicrously called the Battle of the Spurs, the spurs having been more in request than the sword on the occasion. It was during this expedition to France that James IV. of Scotland invaded Henry's dominions. Crossing the border, he laid waste the country to the south of the Tweed, and captured a few castles and small towns. But the earl of Surrey, marching into Northumberland, met him at Flodden field, and in the battle which followed the Scotch were completely defeated. James himself, with his son, and nearly all the chief of the Scottish nobility, were among the slain. The Scotch, indeed, were very unwilling to admit the death of their king, though they confessed that he disappeared during the affray. The popular account was, that he had gone on a pilgrimage to the Holy Land, and the credulous mountaineers long expected the return of their royal chief.

It would now have been easy for Henry to have marched upon Paris. But the pope had gained, in the expulsion of the French from

Italy, all that he wanted from the war, and therefore addressed a flattering letter to Henry, congratulating him on his victories at home and abroad, and counselling him now to desist from his hostilities with France. Leo knew too well, however, the ambitious character of Henry, to suppose that he would abstain altogether from the pursuit of a warrior's renown. He, therefore, suggested to him that there were other enemies against whom he would do well to turn his arms. "God will recompense you," said he, "with much greater honour, if you propose to yourself the termination of your difficulties with your present enemies, and apply yourself to humble the pride, and subdue the ferocity of the Turks. Already the kingdoms of Hungary and Bohemia are harassed and depopulated by their incursions; whilst Italy herself sees these barbarians approaching still nearer, an alarming and a melancholy spectacle."

The French monarch, also, to whom this war had been so disastrous, was desirous of either pacifically ending his differences with Henry, or of forming some alliance to strengthen his own arms. At first, he turned his eyes towards the young archduke Charles, afterwards the emperor Charles v. He thought, that by marrying his daughter to this young prince, he should secure the aid of both his relations, Maximilian of Austria, and Ferdinand of Aragon, and might then safely prosecute his designs upon Milan. But Leo understood his wishes, and saw also the great accessions of power which such a marriage would ultimately give to Charles. Trembling not only for the peace of Italy, but for that of Europe itself, if so many sovereignties should be vested in the hands of one youthful monarch, he determined to prevent the intended union. By his artful representations to Louis, he convinced him that it would be wiser to ally himself with the king of England, than with any continental prince. Accordingly, Louis made proposals of peace to Henry, offering to pay one million of crowns for the expenses of the war, and begging that an alliance might be cemented between the two kingdoms, by a marriage between himself and Henry's youngest sister, the princess Mary. Henry's pride was gratified by both these proposals, and although the French king was fifty-three years of age, and Mary only eighteen, the marriage was soon afterwards effected. Thus the pope succeeded, by his politic measures, in giving peace to the west of Europe; and whatever may be thought of his motives, which were certainly not unselfish or pure, there can be no doubt that the result was permanently good. The wars which had so long raged between the French and English nations, producing such extravagant waste of treasure, and such mournful havoc of human life, were terminated by this alliance, and the excessive and dangerous accumulation of power, which would otherwise have fallen to the ambitious Charles v., was partially directed into other and safer channels.

While Leo was thus busily occupied with the affairs of Europe, he was not inattentive to the wants of Rome and her dependent states. Since the discovery of the art of printing, that city had made less progress than most others in Italy in literature and the fine arts. During the reign of Julius II., who gloried in being "no scholar," the domestic tumults and foreign wars had so multiplied as to drive away all lovers of learning. The university, established nearly a century before, was in a very languishing condition, and Leo's first object was to place it on a firmer footing. He restored its revenues, which had been seized to defray the expenses of war. He appointed numerous professors, some of whom were among the most learned men of the age. He conferred such privileges and immunities on the students as were sure to attract many to the university, and incite them to close application. These efforts were crowned with success. In the very first year of his pontificate, Leo was able to say, "Such numbers of students have resorted to this place, that the university of Rome is likely soon to be held in higher estimation than any other in Italy."

For the cultivation of Greek literature he displayed a still more anxious zeal. Noble Greeks, exiled from their native land, were at that time found in many Italian cities, earning a livelihood by giving instructions in their native tongue. Among these, Giovanni Lascar was one of the most eminent. He had been patronised by Lorenzo de Medici, and was now invited to take up his abode in Rome. By his advice, Leo addressed the following letter to Musurus, another distinguished teacher of the Greek language, then residing at Venice:—

"LEO X. TO MARCUS MUSURUS.

"Having a most earnest desire to promote the study of the Greek language and of Grecian literature, which are now almost extinct, and to encourage the liberal arts as far as lies in my power, and being well convinced of your great learning and singular judgment, I request that you will take the trouble of inviting from Greece ten young men, or as many more as you may think proper, of good education and virtuous dispositions, who may compose a seminary of liberal studies, and from whom the Italians may derive the proper use and knowledge of the Greek tongue. On this subject you will be more fully instructed by Giovanni Lascar, whose virtues and learning have deservedly rendered him dear to me. I have a confidence, also, from the respect and kindness you have already shown me, that you will apply with the utmost diligence to effect what may seem to you to be necessary for accomplishing the purposes which I have in view.

"*August 8th*, 1513."

A Greek seminary was accordingly established in Rome, of which Musurus was, for a short time, the president; receiving from the pope various ecclesiastical appointments in reward. A Greek printing-press was also erected, and Lascar superintended the printing of the works which issued from it. Among the first of these were the Iliad and Odyssey of Homer, and the tragedies of Sophocles, with the notes of the ancient commentators.

In his zeal for the revival of classical learning, Leo published his intention to give large rewards for the discovery of manuscripts of Greek or Roman authors, engaging to print them at his own expense. In consequence of this announcement, the first five books of the Annals of Tacitus, which, until then, had only existed in manuscript, and were exceedingly rare in that form, were brought from the abbey of Corvey, in Westphalia; and soon afterwards, the first complete edition of that historian's works was published at Rome. It was the custom of Leo to grant to the editors of such books the exclusive privilege of reprinting and selling them; and, in bestowing this privilege on Beroaldo, the editor of Tacitus, he justifies himself for the particular attention he bestowed upon classical literature in the following words: " Amongst the other objects of our attention, since we have been raised by Divine goodness to the pontifical dignity, and devoted to the government, and as far as in us lies to the extension of the Christian church, we have considered those pursuits as not the least important, which lead to the promotion of literature and useful arts; for we have been accustomed, even from our early years, to think that nothing more excellent or more useful has been given by the Creator to mankind, if we except only the knowledge and true worship of himself." He then pronounces a sentence of excommunication, with a fine of two hundred ducats, and forfeiture of the books, upon any person reprinting these works within the next ten years.

Much as we must commend the pontiff's zeal for promoting learning, it is impossible to notice, without pain, the marvellous levity with which he employs, for mere secular purposes, these censures of the church, which the priests diligently taught would insure to the censured eternal banishment from the kingdom of heaven.

The attention which Leo paid to the intellectual demands of his age did not, however, prevent his discovering considerable anxiety for the advancement of his own family in honours, power, and wealth. Indeed, the time was now come when efforts for this purpose could be made with good prospect of success. The politic and cautious manner in which the pope had conducted himself towards the other sovereigns of Europe, had secured him the fear of some, and the respect of all. Feeling himself, therefore, in a position to move with advantage, he resolved on a measure so bold, and so inconsistent with his former behaviour, as only to be accounted for by the supposition that he was bent, at all hazards, on the aggrandizement of his house. Hitherto, his opposition had been the most effectual hindrance to the king of France becoming master of the duchy of Milan. But, altering his tactics, Leo now made proposals to Louis to renew his attempts upon that province, assuring him, at the same time, that little resistance was to be feared from either the Swiss or the Spaniards, both of whom were greatly exhausted by the efforts they had already made, and that he himself would give no countenance to such resistance, even if it were attempted. Some have supposed that this strange advice was a mere artifice of the pope's to embroil the French and Spanish sovereigns; but Roscoe, with greater probability, conjectures that Leo's intention was to procure from Louis, in return for the help thus proffered, some similar aid in designs of his own upon the crown of Naples, which he was desirous of placing upon the head of his brother Giuliano. Certain it is, that in the proposals made to Louis both Giuliano and the young Lorenzo are mentioned as parties to the treaty, and it is expressly required that their services to Louis should be duly rewarded. But the worldly and ambitious schemes of the pontiff were thwarted by the death of the French king, in the month of January, 1515.

Florence was now under the government of the youngest of the family, Lorenzo de' Medici. The tranquillity which the citizens enjoyed, enabled them again to indulge that taste for splendid exhibitions and dramatic spectacles, for which the gay city of Florence had long been renowned. To prepare these popular entertainments, the skill of artists famous through the world was often exerted; as was the case, more recently, in France, when the painter David designed and conducted the gorgeous fêtes of the first French revolution. One of these singular spectacles, described by the Florentine historians, was called "The Triumph of Death." This was represented by a car, drawn by black oxen, and painted with figures of skulls and bones. On the top of the car stood a large figure of death, armed with a scythe, and from openings in the side of the vehicle there issued, as often as it stood still, men dressed and painted so as to resemble skeletons, who chanted, to a melancholy tune, the words—

> "Once like you we were,
> Spectres now you see;
> Such as we now are,
> Such you soon shall be."

The whole representation probably had a political meaning, and was intended to alarm the people with apprehensions of being reduced to ruin under the rule of the Medici. But the Medici not only permitted such license to the citizens, they also themselves prepared, at great expense, exhibitions of a similar kind for the amusement of the people, knowing that, by these means, they were likely to be diverted from any serious attempts to regain their freedom. Wishing in one of them to represent "The Triumph of Camillus," after his victory over the Gauls, Lorenzo sent to his uncle Leo, and begged that he would send him an elephant, two leopards, and a panther, which had been presented to the pope by the king of Portugal, for the purpose of their gracing the triumphal procession. The leopards and panther were sent under the care of their Persian keeper; and so great was the excitement created by the entire exhibition, that many of the cardinals and most distinguished officers of the Roman court travelled expressly to Florence to be spectators of the scene. By such methods were the Florentines in some degree reconciled to a political degradation, which they could not but feel to be humiliating and oppressive.

CHAPTER VIII.

Francis I., king of France—Designs the recovery of Milan—Leo dissembles his intentions—Resolves on opposing Francis—Forms an Italian league—Francis enters Italy—Battle of Marignano—Chevalier Bayard—Leo makes overtures to Francis—Francis proposes an interview—Leo passes through Florence—Meets Francis at Bologna—Occurrences on that occasion—Pragmatic Sanction abolished—Wolsey made cardinal—Francis and Leo separate—Death of Giuliano de' Medici.

FRANCIS I. was the successor of Louis XII. on the throne of France. Although as devoid of true Christianity as most of his contemporaries appear unhappily to have been, he yet displayed qualities that entitle him to a more than equal share in the attention which the monarchs of that period claim from posterity. The oracles of God declare that "not many wise men after the flesh, not many mighty, not many noble are called;" and the noble, the mighty, and the wise, of the age of Leo X., furnish numerous exemplifications, but present very few exceptions to this general rule. But in those natural and acquired qualities which usually command the respect and admiration of mankind, Francis was richly endowed. He was brave, courteous, generous, and, as a ruler, for the most part sagacious. Like Henry VIII., however, he was inflamed with the desire of conquest, and he therefore lost no time in re-asserting the right of the French crown to the sovereignty of Milan. But, more prudent than his predecessor, he resolved, before attempting an invasion, to strengthen himself by alliance with other powers. To the king of England he engaged to pay forthwith the million of crowns which Louis had promised but never sent, and Henry agreed, on this condition, to renew the treaty already existing. Francis also endeavoured to secure the friendship of the emperor Maximilian, and that of Ferdinand of Aragon, but in this he failed of success. The Venetians, however, expressed a readiness to co-operate with him against Milan, whenever he should cross the Italian frontier.

It was of still more consequence to Francis to obtain the assistance of the pope, but Leo was far too cautious to give countenance to such a project without mature deliberation. It may, perhaps, be fairly assumed, that he would have preferred, had it been possible, to keep the French altogether out of Italy. On the other hand, he could see that, if they should secure a footing in Milan, their power would be a considerable check to the ambition of the young archduke Charles, whenever he should ascend the Spanish throne. He accordingly temporized, and acted with no little artifice and disingenuousness. To what extent his dissimulation was carried, and in what esteem he was held on account of the line of conduct he adopted on this occasion, may be inferred from a passage in a letter addressed to him, about this time, by Fregoso, the doge of Genoa. Fregoso had treacherously offered to betray Genoa into the hands of the French king, and his design being discovered, he attempts to justify himself to the pope by saying, that as Leo's "penetration must have perceived that the measures which he had adopted were such as seemed necessary for the preservation of his authority, any further excuse must be superfluous, it being well understood that it was allowable, or at least customary, for a sovereign to resort to expedients of an extraordinary nature, not only for the preservation, but even for the increase of his dominions; although he well knew it would be difficult to apologize for his conduct, if he were addressing himself to a prince who considered matters of state by those rules of morality which are only applicable to private life." We may not be surprised at the prevalence of such grossly immoral doctrines, at a time when the "Prince" of Machiavelli was the code of morals among rulers; but it was, indeed, a fearful symptom of wide-spread irreligion, and ominous of the speedy downfall of the papal authority, that such language could be addressed, and such principles be imputed, without rebuke or contradiction, to the nominal head of the Christian church.

After much hesitation, the pope determined on offering resistance to the threatened invasion; but, aware of the uncertain result of the struggle, he conducted all his measures in such a way as to give the least possible offence to the French king. Quietly he collected together all the forces which Italy could furnish to the cause. Allies were not wanting, but they were mostly of doubtful value. Besides the levies of the Milanese, raised by the duke's most strenuous efforts, the Spanish general, Cardona, brought twelve thousand men; Lorenzo de' Medici commanded nearly three thousand of Florentine troops; and three thousand Roman cavalry, with a large body of infantry, took the field under Giuliano, the brother of the pope, who had been appointed general of the church. But by far the most formidable foes to the designs of Francis were the Swiss, who, feeling exasperated that a large sum of money, promised them by Louis XII. in the previous campaign, had not been paid, threatened to obstruct the march of the French army, and soon afterwards, to the number of thirty-five thousand, descending from their mountains, joined their arms with those of the Italian and Spanish allies. Could these various armies have been wholly depended on, and had they been led by some commander of competent ability, they would, doubtless, easily have repulsed the French invader from the plains of Italy. But mutual distrust, and the selfish aims of the several leaders, rendered the entire armament powerless before the discipline and valour of their opponents.

The army of Francis amounted to upwards

of thirty thousand soldiers, and was not only one of the largest, but among the best equipped and trained that modern Europe had then seen. The king displayed his generalship in the first step he took. Instead of crossing the Alps by the route then usual, from Grenoble to Susa, where the Milanese forces awaited his approach, he made a circuit to the south, and passed through defiles at that time rarely trodden, and so difficult to his troops, that they were often obliged to hew pathways through the solid rock, and let down the ponderous artillery from crag to crag. By this means, however, he reached the banks of the Po without obstruction, and while the Milanese general, Colonna, was feasting with his officers, wholly unsuspicious of the progress the enemy had made, Francis suddenly attacked him in the rear, and made him prisoner, together with many of his attendants.

This disaster so discouraged the allies, that they were incapable of making any vigorous efforts to resist the French king's further advance. The Swiss alone, partly from a thirst for victory, and partly from a hope of booty, were resolved to withstand his march. When Francis arrived at Marignano, in the territory of Milan, he found them already encamped there, and on this spot both parties were determined that the fate of Italy should be decided. For several days the armies continued within sight of each other, without either daring to begin the assault. At length the Swiss, after listening to an inflammatory harangue from the cardinal of Sion, who had accompanied them to the war, resolved on giving battle immediately, although it was within two hours of sunset. Rushing with impetuous speed on the French camp, they threw the whole army into confusion by their unexpected attack. But the French were too brave to fly, or to yield without a contest. Gradually recovering from their surprise, and marshalling their forces, they maintained a firm resistance till far into the night. Darkness compelled the combatants to desist, but they remained under arms all night. At dawn of day the Swiss discovered that Francis had availed himself of the interval to arrange his troops in better order, and especially so to place his artillery as to commit terrible havoc on their lines. Nevertheless, they advanced boldly to the conflict, and continued it with desperate resolution for several hours. But towards noon, the Venetian allies of Francis, under the fierce D'Alviano, joined the French army, and rushing into the midst of the affray, raised the cry of "Marco," the war signal of the Venetians; and the Swiss, feeling that they were too exhausted to cope with this new enemy, relinquished the contest, and retired in good order, but leaving upwards of ten thousand dead upon the field.

The victory had not been purchased without severe losses also on the side of the French. Trivulzio, one of the Italian allies of Francis, declared that, although he had been in eighteen pitched battles, they all resembled the play of children in comparison with this, which might justly be styled a war of giants. Francis himself, writing to his mother, Louisa, affirms that so sanguinary and ferocious a battle had not been fought for more than two thousand years. It was in this terrible strife of arms, also, that the celebrated Bayard, "the knight without fear and without reproach," fought by the side of the French king, and performed such romantic prodigies of valour, that Francis, struck with his bravery, insisted on receiving at his hands the honour of knighthood. The king kneeled down before the valiant soldier, who, laying his sword upon the monarch's shoulder, bade him arise a true knight of chivalry. Bayard himself, overjoyed at the honour done him, gave two leaps in the air, and, returning his sword to its scabbard, vowed that it should never more be unsheathed except against the Turks, the Saracens, or the Moors. How lamentable that such qualities should have been so perverted! How much more admirable would the courage and energy discovered by Bayard appear to us, had they been devoted to the warfare of Christian soldiership, and employed in risking life for the cause of Christ and the salvation of men, instead of being prostituted to deeds of carnage, and the furtherance of unrighteous schemes of conquest!

Already had the wily pope made preparations for conciliating Francis, should the necessity arise. It was in compliance with his will that the Florentine and Roman armies had abstained from all interference in the battle of Marignano. Now that the result of that conflict was known, Leo lost no time in sending his confidential servant, Lodovico Canossa, to offer his alliance to the conqueror. Happily for the pope, Francis was not unwilling to consent to such a proposal. He knew, from the example of Louis, that even when the temporal power of the pope was annihilated, he still swayed a potent spiritual sceptre. He was quite ready to avoid the inconvenience and vexations of an interdict. He accordingly gave the papal envoy a gracious reception, and suggested that the negotiations might more easily be settled, if a personal meeting were to take place between himself and the pope. To this proposition the pontiff very gladly consented, no doubt conceiving that, by availing himself of his natural courtesy of address and eloquence of speech, he might turn the interview to advantageous account. The city of Bologna was appointed for the place of meeting, as Leo was by no means desirous that the youthful conqueror should advance so far as Rome.

The pope directed the cardinals and prelates residing in Rome and the neighbouring cities to join him on the way, and towards the end of November, attended by a large and splendid retinue, departed for Bologna. His route lay through Florence, and when the citizens knew that they were to be honoured with the pope's presence, they made unexampled preparations to receive him in becoming state. On approaching his native town, Leo found the gates and part of the walls thrown down to admit him, and a triumphal arch erected, richly sculptured with historical scenes and emblems, beneath which he was to pass. In adorning every part of the city, the resources of art had been lavishly expended. Triumphal arches and columns, statues and busts, by the most eminent sculptors, met the eye in every direction. The church of S. Maria del Fiore was a particular object of attention. The entire face of the edifice was decorated with statues and figures in relief, besides scenes painted in chiaroscuro by the pencil of Andrea del Sarto, so that Leo declared the structure could not have appeared more beautiful had it been built of marble. Several days were passed at Florence in festivities, after which Leo continued his journey.

At Bologna his reception was far different. The courtesies required on state occasions were paid by the proper functionaries, but there were no greetings from the people, no signs of welcome voluntarily displayed. Three days later the arrival of Francis was announced, and a procession of cardinals and bishops met him at the gates, and saluted him with the fraternal kiss. The pope, arrayed in his pontifical robes, expected him in the state apartments of the palace, and at length Francis made his appearance, between two cardinals. He was attended by a multitude of followers, and the building was so filled with the populace, both Roman and French, that he was more than half an hour in making his way through the crowd. Arriving in the presence of the pope, Francis first knelt and kissed his foot, then saluted his hand, and lastly his face. After various complimentary orations, the ceremonies were concluded by the admission of the French nobility to the honour of kissing the feet of the pope, who then laid aside the robes of state, and entered into familiar conversation. The king was anxious to obtain several concessions from the pope, demands which the latter dexterously parried by fair speeches and magnificent presents. Among the latter were two worthy of distinct mention. To Francis, Leo gave a large cross, richly ornamented with jewels, worth fifteen thousand ducats; and to the beautiful Maria Gaudin he presented a diamond of immense value, and which has ever since been called the Gaudin diamond.

One important arrangement was made, however, on this occasion, which involved both a sacrifice of power and a violation of duty on the part of the pope, according to the principles of the papacy. The French clergy had for ages claimed the right of managing their own affairs, independently for the most part of papal control. The popes had as strenuously resisted the claim. But an assembly of prelates and priests who met at Bourges during the reign of Charles VII., and styled themselves the Pragmatic Council, had sanctioned this claim, and decreed that the right should be permanently enjoyed. Under this authority, known as the Pragmatic Sanction, the clergy of France had become in a great measure independent alike of the pope and of the king, and in many instances had given considerable umbrage to both. Francis now solicited the pope's consent to the transfer of all jurisdiction in ecclesiastical affairs, without appeal, to himself and his successors on the throne. Leo, on his part, was willing to humble the pride of the contumacious clergy, and as it was impossible for him to exercise the power to which his predecessors had vainly asserted a right, he consented that the kings of France should thenceforth, with a few exceptions, preside over church as well as state, and appoint to all benefices which had previously been in the gift of the Romish see. This procedure sets in the strongest light the levity with which the most sacred offices had come to be regarded, even by those who stood pledged to maintain them in the highest degree of purity and vigour. When the nominal head of the church could thus recklessly barter his high functions for political profit, the time could not be far distant for some bold spirit to arise, who should vividly portray the contrast between the simplicity and self-denial of the apostles, and the cupidity of their self-styled successors. It was Leo and his fraternity who awakened the genius of Luther.

Among the minor, yet interesting results of this conference between Francis and the pope, was the presentation of a cardinal's hat to the famous Wolsey, then archbishop of York. A fierce dispute had been raging for some time between Wolsey and Louis Guillard, a favourite of Francis I., both of whom laid claim to the bishopric of Tournay. Francis hoped both to please his ally, the English king, and to secure the bishopric for his own servant, by gratifying the ambition of Wolsey, and therefore besought of the pope his elevation to the rank of cardinal. Leo granted the request, but the haughty priest was not to be bribed into silence, and in no degree relaxed his efforts to obtain the bishopric for himself.

The French monarch had now accomplished his objects in the invasion of Italy, and on quitting Bologna, he rapidly passed through his Milanese territory, and soon afterwards repassed the Alps. Leo returned to Florence, and thence to Rome, whither the tidings followed him that his brother Giuliano had expired at Florence, in the month of March, 1516. Giuliano's history is throughout subordinate to that of the pope, and his character, though esteemed for general goodness of intention, was too undecided to permit of his leaving an illustrious name. It has been justly observed, that "the noble monument erected to his memory by Michel Angelo, in the chapel of S. Lorenzo at Florence, may be considered as the most durable memorial of his fame."

CHAPTER IX.

Leo's ambitious designs—Seizes on the state of Urbino—Pretence for it in the character of the duke—The duke expelled—Recovers his possessions—Leo demands aid of all Christendom—The duke abdicates—Injustice of the pope, which contains the seeds of retribution—Its success owing to the superstition of the age—Conspiracy of the cardinals against the pope — Confession and execution of some—Leniency of Leo towards others—Thirty-one new cardinals—Leo's general government.

To sovereigns who are not hereditary there are, unquestionably, strong temptations to abuse their tenure of power for purposes of mere family aggrandizement; and the popes have ever been distinguished by earnest zeal and persevering effort to accomplish this object. Hence there has often been more unjust and illegal oppression under the papal government, than even under the unchristian despotisms of the east. The family of the Medici was of too aspiring a character for Leo to escape the general contagion of his class; and the death of his brother Giuliano led him to the adoption of measures, that seriously affect his reputation for justice and honour. Giuliano had always been regarded by the pontiff with much affection, and no opportunity was neglected of advancing his interests. It is highly probable that Leo's ambition aimed at nothing less than placing the crown of Naples on his brother's head. But now Lorenzo, his nephew, was the only member of his family through whom he could hope to perpetuate the power and rank which it had so long enjoyed in Italy. Lorenzo was, on his part, sufficiently ambitious and unscrupulous to second his uncle's endeavours on his behalf, whatever direction they might take.

Francesco Maria del Rovere, duke of Urbino, had long been an object of resentment to Leo on various accounts. Under the pontificate of Julius II., his uncle, the duke had acted as general of the papal troops, and when the Medici were restored to Florence, he so far displayed his hostility to their cause, as to refuse obedience to the pope's mandate to give them all the support in his power. Again, after the battle of Ravenna, he had denied admission to the Roman soldiers, who, at the gates of Urbino, implored protection from their pursuers. But, although resentment and ambition were the motives which now actuated the pontiff, he took care to conceal them under a profession of zeal for the church and religion. He accused the duke of treachery, of contumacy to the see of Rome, and of not fulfilling his promises to supply the funds which it was his duty to contribute to the church. He also reminded him of many crimes which he had perpetrated in the course of a long military life. Among these, the principal was, the assassination of the cardinal of Pavia. In the wars of Julius II., the cardinal had been intrusted with the protection of Bologna. Not receiving the support which he needed from the duke of Urbino, and which, as general of the church, he was bound to afford, the cardinal abandoned the city to the French, and hastened to excuse himself to the pope by exposing the negligence of the duke. The duke, however, met him on the way, as he was passing through the streets of Ravenna, in the midst of his guards. The soldiers respectfully ranged themselves on each side to allow the duke to pass; but he, riding between their ranks, approached the cardinal, and stabbed him with his dagger, so that he instantly fell dead from his horse. The memory of this atrocious deed was now revived by Leo, and formed part of the charge which he urged against the duke, as a ground for dispossessing him of the estate of Urbino.

The first step taken by the pope was to summon the duke to Rome, that he might undergo a judicial examination. But Francesco was well acquainted with the common result of such inquiries, and, instead of complying with the summons, he fled to Mantua, where the marquis, his father-in-law, resided. As a rebel to the church, he was then formally excommunicated, and Leo gave orders that Lorenzo de' Medici should march at the head of fourteen thousand men, and take possession of the duchy. The conquest was easily effected, as few of the towns and fortresses were in a condition to resist. But the castle of St. Leon was so well garrisoned, and so securely situated on the top of a lofty and precipitous rock, as to be able to support a siege for three months. It was at length taken by stratagem. A master carpenter having ascended the steepest part of the rock by night, fixed the ladders of the besiegers, so that a number of them scaled the walls, and the garrison, supposing themselves betrayed, or that the place was stormed, immediately opened the gates.

Lorenzo de' Medici was forthwith invested with the dukedom, and the exiled duke, finding it vain to hope for restoration at present, contented himself with earnestly beseeching the pope to remove from him the spiritual censures of the church. But to this moderate request the pontiff turned a deaf ear, although the duke implored it " for the salvation of his soul ;" on which incident, so characteristic of the times, of the haughtiness that reigned among the clergy, and of the superstition that prevailed with the laity, Roscoe strikingly remarks : " Thus the man, who appears to have felt no remorse for the assassination of another, and that, too, a cardinal of the church, professed his anxiety in labouring under the displeasure of the pope ; and thus the pontiff, to whom the care of all Christendom was intrusted, after despoiling the object of his resentment of all his possessions in this world, refused to pardon him even in the next."

The peaceful state of Italy at this juncture, enabled the duke Francesco to raise, in a short time, a numerous army. Aided by Spanish soldiers and French stipendiaries, besides the forces which the marquis of Mantua could bring into the field, he marched rapidly upon his own dominions, and taking Lorenzo as much by surprise as he himself had been before, he entered the city of Urbino unopposed, and reinstated himself in his palace, Lorenzo being absent at the neighbouring town of Cesena.

It was impossible for the pope immediately to array against the duke a sufficient force to eject him from the duchy. But, with twofold resources, he had quick recourse to his spiritual authority, and demanded the aid of all Christian princes in punishing a rebel to the church. This demand he especially pressed upon the Spanish and French sovereigns, whose soldiers were now in the pay of the duke of Urbino. He also forwarded it to the English monarch, Henry VIII. Neither the French nor the Spanish court was inclined to incur the interdict of the pope. It was much easier to sacrifice a petty Italian duke, however just his cause. From each of them, accordingly, a command was issued to those officers and soldiers who had followed the duke of Urbino, to withdraw from his army. A considerable number of troops was also sent by both sovereigns to the assistance of Leo. By Francis I., indeed, some objections were made to the cruelty the pope had exercised, but he at the same time expressly recognised Lorenzo de' Medici as the duke of Urbino.

With an army strangely composed of Germans, Swiss, Gascons, Spaniards, and Italians, Lorenzo now took the field; and the duke of Urbino immediately discovered apprehensions of an unfavourable result to the contest, by sending heralds to Lorenzo with the proposal, that the dispute should be settled by personal combat between themselves. This message Lorenzo regarded as an insult, and committed the bearers of it to prison. Skirmishes subsequently took place, some fortresses were captured by the papal army, but no general engagement was fought, each general hoping to weary his adversary by delay. In one of these affrays a serious accident occurred, which threatened at once to terminate the quarrel, and the life of one of the leaders. In attacking the castle of St. Costanza, Lorenzo, contrary to the earnest advice of his officers, approached near to the walls, that he might direct the planting of some artillery. On retiring, he was struck by a ball on the back part of the head, and so severely wounded that he was unable to remain with the army.

The cardinal Giulio de' Medici hastened from Rome to assume the command, and the campaign continued for some time longer, without any decisive action taking place. At length, the duke finding his resources nearly exhausted, made proposals for accommodation. The terms of this treaty were, on the part of the duke, the abandonment of all claims to the duchy, and on the part of Leo, the removal of all ecclesiastical censures, together with permission for the mother and wife of the duke to enjoy their own possessions in the state of Urbino, and for himself to remove whatever furniture and books he might wish to carry with him into exile.

But, although the pope had accomplished the object of his ambition, the conquest of Urbino was dearly purchased. His procedures were universally condemned, and throughout Italy excited disgust for his soldiers, his commanders, and his states. So loud was the voice of popular execration, that the design could never have succeeded, had it not been for the superstitious veneration in which the pope's authority was held. This alone prevented the Italian states from succouring the injured duke, and this only induced the monarchs of Europe to sanction so disgraceful a deed. It is worthy of remark, that the occurrences here related, and their consequences, furnish examples of what may frequently be seen, that sins contain within themselves the seeds of retribution. Not only did the duke herein suffer the penalty of his own murderous injustice, but Leo's crime was the germ from which sprang the abundant fruit of Rome's overthrow. The treasury of the church was exhausted by so lengthened a contest, and the poverty thus induced necessitated that sale of indulgences which paved the way for the great Reformation.

Meantime Leo had passed through imminent

peril in his domestic life. Some severities which he had used towards the noble family of the Petrucci so roused the resentment of the cardinal Alfonso, whose kindred they were, that he meditated nothing less than the assassination of the pope. To effect his design, he engaged the services of Battista da Vercelli, a celebrated surgeon in Rome. The pope was at this time afflicted with a disorder which required surgical attendance, and the cardinal Petrucci proposed that, during the absence from home of Leo's own surgeon, Battista should be introduced to him, and should mingle poison with the dressings that it was needful to apply. From this snare, however, the pope escaped, by declining, through a feeling of delicacy, to admit a strange practitioner. But Petrucci's anger burned so fiercely, that he could not endure any delay, and recklessly vented his ill-will to the pope in expressions which were afterwards carried to his ears. He consequently caused Petrucci to be apprehended, together with the cardinal De Sauli, Battista, and some others, who were suspected of confederacy in the plot. The rigorous examination they underwent elicited some confessions suggestive of a yet wider conspiracy, in which several of the cardinals were concerned. Leo therefore determined to call a meeting in full consistory, when the matter might be thoroughly investigated. He previously took care to secure also the person of the cardinal Rafaelle Riario, who had been accused by the other prisoners of being a confederate. Sending for the cardinal to attend the consistory, Leo awaited his coming in an antechamber, guarded by two soldiers and the captain of the palace. When the cardinal entered the room, with a cheerful air, unconscious of danger, the pope, usually so self-possessed and deliberate, but now agitated and pale, hastily walked out, and shutting the door, left the cardinal under arrest.

The cardinals being assembled, the pontiff addressed them on the heinousness of the crime to which some of them had been parties. He then called upon them, in succession, to answer upon oath whether they were innocent or guilty. Francesco Soderini and Adrian di Corneto at first denied any knowledge of the plot, but being pressed to speak the truth, they fell prostrate before the pope, and, with many tears, confessed their crime. These, avowing themselves penitent, were merely sentenced to pay a heavy fine; but the cardinal Petrucci, with his instruments, the surgeon Battista and his private secretary, were strangled in prison, the two latter having first been cruelly tortured. The cardinal De Sauli was condemned to perpetual imprisonment, but was afterwards liberated on the payment of a fine; and the cardinal Riario received a still lighter punishment, and was restored entirely to favour before the expiration of the year.

But, while the execution of these traitors had removed some enemies from the court of Leo, he was well aware that others would spring up from among their families, to revenge their death. He resolved, therefore, to fortify himself against future intrigues, by raising a large number of his friends to the dignity of the purple robe. In one day, he created thirty-one cardinals, among whom a considerable number belonged to his own family or near connexions. Some of them, indeed, were men eminent for their talent or learning, but these qualities were evidently not of chief consideration. Others belonged to the royal houses of Europe, and owed their elevation to the expectation of the pope to receive a suitable return.

The measure, viewed only as a political one, was undoubtedly well-advised. Hitherto, the reign of Leo had been distracted both by foreign invasions and domestic feuds; but, from this period to the close of his life, the stream of events in Italy flowed calm and smooth. The new cardinals of princely and noble houses flocked to reside at Rome, and brought with them the rich revenues of the sees, monasteries, and other preferments which they held in far distant lands. Their wealth circulated through the city, and considerably promoted the prosperity of its inhabitants. Leo also gave a new impulse to trade by abolishing various monopolies, and by encouraging the settlement of merchants, whose business attracted to Rome the commodities of the world. This period was justly regarded by the Romans as one of the most prosperous their city had known since the downfall of the ancient empire.

CHAPTER X.

A reformation become necessary — General licentiousness, especially of the clergy—First effects of the revival of literature—Vices of the priesthood exposed — Dante — Petrarch—Boccaccio—Attempt to check these exposures—Philosophical studies discouraged—Atheistic habits of the clergy—Utter disregard of morality—Leo's own habits of life—Europe prepared for reformation—Simultaneous outbreak in various countries—England and Wycliffe—Switzerland and Zwingle—France and Lefèvre and Farel—Germany and Reuchlin, Erasmus, and Luther—Luther's early life—Visit to Rome—Disgust at its profligate manners.

THE history of Leo the Tenth has already furnished us with many proofs that a reformation, both in religion and in manners, was loudly called for. For ages had the general depravity advanced, and the remonstrances of the few intrepid men, a Huss or a Wycliffe, who, at intervals lifted up their voices against it, had only served to discover, by their utter failure, its increasing strength. In the lives of Alexander VI. and his son, Cæsar Borgia, we behold with amazement what lengths of iniquity were dared with impunity, even by men who occupied the most conspicuous stations in the church and in the state. We have seen dignified ecclesiastics plotting against the life of their sovereign, and acknowledged spiritual chief. And if such were the deeds of the noblest in rank, we shall hardly expect to find a more particular observance of morality among their inferiors. That the clergy of all classes were guilty of the most corrupt and licentious conduct is sufficiently attested by the single fact, that in the eleventh session of the Lateran Council, held under the pontificate of Leo, there is express reference made to a custom as being prevalent with the priesthood, of both living themselves in open impurity, and even making gain by permitting the same practice to others.

Since the revival of letters, indeed, these crimes had been somewhat more severely exposed and condemned. So early as the close of the thirteenth century, the poet Dante had expressed himself with just indignation against the vices of those who ought to have been patterns of holiness, and in such stirring strains that he brought down upon his head the malice and persecution of many powerful foes. In the first part of his celebrated poem, "The Divine Comedy," in which he describes his descent into the abodes of the lost, he represents himself as meeting with prelates, and even popes, enduring the most excruciating torments. Thus, having plunged to the fourth circle in that horrible pit, where the avaricious and prodigal receive their punishment, he finds the wretched beings condemned eternally to push forward at their breasts enormous loads, and meeting half-way in the circuit with their brethren in misery, furiously clashing their burdens; then, recoiling from the tremendous shock, they vent their wrath on each other in abusive epithets. The poet, inquiring who those were with shaven heads, is told—

> "Priests once, both popes and cardinals were they,
> Whose heads, uncovered, are devoid of hair;
> O'er them foul avarice held unbounded sway."
> CANTO vii.

Pursuing his downward journey, the poet reaches the seventh circle, where he beholds the blasphemers against God, suffering the penalty of their impiety. On a hot, sandy plain, some are stretched prostrate upon the burning soil, some twisted convulsively in the most hideous distortions, and some pacing hurriedly to and fro, but all incessantly beating off with their hands large flakes of fire, which fall

> "Like snow,
> On Alpine summits, when the wind is low."

And, asking their history, he learns that these

> "All were *priests*, and in their time
> Great literati, not unknown to fame,
> On earth polluted with the self-same crime."
> CANTO xiv.

Passing over many other allusions which Dante makes, in the course of the same poem, to the vicious and profligate lives of the clergy, we find him, in the nineteenth canto, pouring forth a torrent of indignant scorn upon the pope then reigning, Boniface VIII. and his predecessor, Nicholas III., both of whom were notorious for their greedy sale, to the highest bidder, of offices in the church.

A bank pierced with holes is the prison house of those convicted of simony. In these holes, the criminals are inextricably fixed in an inverted position, only their feet and legs being visible above. Scorching flames rage around their feet, so that the legs ceaselessly quiver in violent agony. The poet arrives at the lower side of the bank, where the head of one of the sufferers can be seen, and discovers it to be that of the late pope, Nicholas III. The miserable shade perceiving his visitor, and supposing him to be Boniface, who was destined to be his successor in both worlds, accosts him :

"'What! Art thou come, and upright too?' he cried,
'Art thou arrived, and upright, Boniface?'"

His error being corrected, and learning that his visitor is a mortal, travelling by permission of Heaven through these strange regions in quest of information, Nicholas then explains to the poet the nature of his crime, and receives from him in return a condemnation as just as it is severe. These lines, which were evidently intended to apply to the reigning pontiff, show in a striking manner the intense abhorrence which Dante felt for the profligate avarice of the nominal ministers of religion, and the marvellous courage with which he dared to unmask their hypocrisy :—

"To you Saint John referred, O shepherds vile,
  When She, who sits on many waters, had
  Been seen with kings her person to defile.
    *   *   *   *   *
Your gods you made of silver and of gold,
  And wherein differ from idolaters,
Save that their god is one, but yours a hundred-fold?"

The earnest and deprecatory spirit of Dante communicated some of its ardour to others; and at a later period, Petrarch, the idol of his age, crowned in the Capitol by the hands of nobles, did not hesitate to reprehend the vices of the clergy with the severest censures. In one of his sonnets, he compares the papal court to Babylon, affirming it to be " the residence ot misery, and the mother of error ;" and in another, he uses the strongest epithets he can select, to express his horror and disgust at the profligacy tolerated in the high places of religion.

But of all these early writers, it is probable that Boccaccio produced the greatest effect. The profligate stories of the " Decameron" portray, in vivid colours, the licentiousness of the times, and show that those who filled sacred offices, by no means laid aside the debaucheries of the laity with their costume. This work was, of course, the more influential, because of the popular form in which it was written. Multitudes could laugh at the witty jest levelled at the clergy by Boccaccio, to whom the sublime conceptions and stern admonitions of Dante must have been either unintelligible or dull.

Between these writers and the advent of Lorenzo de' Medici to the supreme power in Florence, a long and dark interval elapsed. The vices of the people increased, and there was little even of intellectual light to dissipate the general gloom; and during the life of Lorenzo, although under his fostering protection men of genius and learning multiplied, there was small sympathy felt for any amendment in morals; and a reformer like Savonarola was far more likely to be scoffed at for his fanaticism, than commended for his pious, though eccentric and often misguided zeal. The conduct of the Roman pontiffs was that of men whose destruction was foreshadowed by their insane folly; for, instead of promptly correcting the evils that were pointed out—thus at once conciliating the objector, and remedying the disease which preyed upon their church—it was their uniform practice to silence, excommunicate, and persecute any who ventured to arraign the priesthood at the bar of public opinion. It was ever their ruinous policy to check inquiries that threatened, in the least degree, to weaken the authority they held.

It was on similar ground that philosophical studies were discouraged, if not wholly prohibited. Under Lorenzo, the writings of Plato had supplanted those of Aristotle in the favour of literary men, and the philosophy of the Academy began to triumph over that of the Lycæum. The creed of the learned became a strange mixture of Platonism and Christianity, which, of course, tended to the entire extinction of practical religion. Those writers rose to the highest popularity who could array the simple doctrines of the Bible in the most graceful philosophical, and even heathenish garb. The infection spread to the pulpit, and the common people were harangued in orations adorned with illustrations, and even arguments, derived from the ancient mythology. Erasmus tells of a sermon which he heard preached before Julius II., in which the orator compared Christ's sufferings and death with those of eminent heroes of ancient times. He referred to Curtius, who devoted himself to death for his country's good; to Socrates, and others, who were innocent victims of malignant cruelty; and in speaking of the pope, he represented him as Jupiter, grasping the lightning in his hand, and swaying the universe by his nod—a comparison which that imperious and aspiring pontiff was tolerably sure to admire.

The impiety of these practices was either unperceived, or not objected to. Leo himself was partial to them. But the zealous study of classical authors, especially those who discoursed on philosophy, soon began to produce other results, far more alarming to the priestly holders of power. Without a firm or intelligent faith in the Scriptures, men were led to the doctrines of Plato and others, as affording some solid ground for their belief. The mummeries of the Romish church were despised, and the authority of the pope was in danger of being utterly contemned. To check this spirit of insubordination, a decree was passed in the Lateran Council for restraining the study of philosophy among the clergy, and wholly preventing the publication of any doctrines subversive of those taught by the papal church. Such measures could never hinder the growth of infidelity, although they might compel its concealment.

As disbelief in the teachings of the Romish church thus gained an ascendency over the hearts of men, their lives became more dissolute than ever. The manners of the Roman citizens at this period were too gross to admit of particular description. An illustration or two may, however, be ventured on. Cardinal Bembo, chief secretary to the pope, and one of the most distinguished ecclesiastics of his time, lived in open and unreproved sin. Molza, a native of Modena, came to Rome, and becoming a popular poet, and a great favourite of Leo X., passed a life less devoted to poetry than to impure gratifications. Forsaking his own wife, he indulged in licentiousness, which nearly cost him his life, as it provoked an attempt at his assassination, and it was only with great difficulty that he recovered from his wounds. Crimes of the same description followed in succession, and he at length died from the effect of his debaucheries. Another of Leo's favourites was the notorious Peter Aretino, whose writings are a disgrace to humanity, the vilest of a vile age, and whose death was in melancholy keeping with his abandoned life, for, hearing an account of some enormous act of depravity committed by his sisters, who were women of bad character at Venice, he was seized with such a violent fit of laughter, that he fell backwards upon the floor, and received an injury which quickly resulted in death.

Leo himself passed his days in a perpetual round of pleasure and luxurious living. His banquets were prodigally expensive, rivalling in their delicacies and their splendour those of the ancient emperors. All were welcome at his table who could promote conviviality and mirth. Extemporaneous ballads were often sung or chanted during the feast, and if they contained a moderate proportion of wit, their licentiousness was easily forgiven. Regardless of everything but enjoyment, Leo cared little whether religion decayed or flourished, whether infidelity diminished or increased, provided the revenues were regularly forthcoming to supply the demands made upon his purse by his amusements, his entertainments, and his extravagant gifts. It is even said, that he was so utterly devoid of religious principle, that on one occasion he exclaimed, "How profitable has this fable of Christ been to us!" And although his defenders assert that this story is not well authenticated, yet they themselves record that, when visiting the church of the Annunciation at Florence, he professed to have scruples whether he should withdraw a curtain that concealed an image of the virgin Mary, and that, having consulted the cardinals present, he concluded at last to withdraw it reverently at three short intervals! Either these scruples were real or pretended, and as it is impossible to suspect Leo of superstition, there can be no doubt that the act was one of hypocrisy, to delude the populace, by professing a veneration which he could not feel.

The condition of Italy was, in a large measure, that of all Christendom. In every country, the corruptness of the priesthood had brought the papacy into discredit; whilst the spread of learning by means of the printing-press had diffused an eager, and in no wise friendly spirit of inquiry into all claims of supremacy, like that set up by the pope. In England, the intrepid and impetuous Wycliffe, a century before, had declaimed against the abuses of the Romish church; and his followers, under the name of Lollards, still existed, and often proved thorns in the sides of the priests. In Switzerland, a reformer arose, whose success and fame will bear comparison with Luther's. For more than a hundred years there had been differences between the Swiss and their Romish teachers of religion; the latter ever insisting on a degree of authority, to which the bold spirit of the mountaineers could never be brought to yield. Among the soldiers in the Swiss army, engaged by Leo to oppose the invasion of Francis I., was Zwingle, parish priest or pastor of the congregation of Glaris, in the canton of the Grisons; for in those days it was not unusual for the ministers of religion to wield the sword, especially in defence of the church, and at the bidding of the pope. Zwingle had in his youth heard at Basel the preaching of Wittembach, the friend of Reuchlin, who declared that a time of great changes was at hand, and also proclaimed the death of Christ to be the sole ransom for sin. The heart of Zwingle was greatly impressed by his preaching, and he began seriously to study the word of God. When, afterwards, he accompanied the Swiss troops to Italy, he had an opportunity of seeing more fully the dissipation of the monks, with the pride and luxury of the prelates. He returned to his charge after the disastrous battle of Marignano, more dissatisfied than ever with the state of religion. His eyes were now opened to the meaning of the truths which he had formerly heard from Wittembach; he became himself a preacher of Christ crucified, instead of salvation through ceremonies and penances. Some, seeing the likeness between his views and Luther's, supposed that Zwingle borrowed them from the German. But Zwingle often said, "I began to preach the gospel in the year of grace 1516, that is to say, at a time when the name of Luther had not yet been pronounced in our territories." When the monk Samson came selling indulgences in Switzerland, as Tetzel did in Germany, he found in Zwingle so determined and formidable an opponent, that he carefully avoided him, and went elsewhere with his merchandise.

Equally spontaneous was the rise of the Reformation in France. In the year 1510, a youth, named William Farel, arrived in Paris, for the purpose of studying at the university. He was of a noble family, who lived in one of the valleys on the French slopes of the Cottian

Alps. During his boyhood, much had been said in his village in praise of the young Bayard, who had gone forth from the same district, and so greatly signalized himself in the wars. Farel's father was anxious that he, too, should become a soldier; but he was fond of books, and his spirit recoiled from the rough and dissipated life of camps. On entering the university, he found among the doctors one named Lefèvre, of more devout mind and greater learning than the rest, who frequently deplored the corruptness of the age, and foretold that a great revolution in religion must soon take place. Lefèvre and Farel were mutually attracted to each other, and in course of time became strongly attached. The doctor was composing a book containing legends of the saints, and he was also studying, with considerable zeal, the Holy Scriptures in the original tongues. While thus engaged, D'Aubigné tells us, "one of those sudden gleams which come from on high threw light into his soul. He could no longer suppress those risings of disgust which every Christian heart must feel for childish superstitions. The grandeur of God's word made him sensible that these fables were wretched indeed. That moment was the commencement of a new era in France, and originated the Reformation." Lefèvre continued his studies, and made many disciples, besides Farel, to his now purified faith. He openly taught in the Sorbonne, "that it is God alone who, by his grace, through faith, justifies for everlasting life." When, in 1520, Luther's doctrines were first publicly discussed in Paris, there was a numerous party already formed, well prepared to defend them, of whom Lefèvre, Farel, Briçonnet, bishop of Meaux, and the princess Margaret, sister of Francis I., were the most distinguished.

But Germany was the field of battle in which the reformed faith was to gain its first victories. Some progress in learning had been made by the "barbarous Germans," as the Italians contemptuously styled them, before the appearance of Reuchlin, Erasmus, and Luther; but it was by them that the fountains of sacred knowledge were unsealed, and made accessible to the people. So early as 1498, Reuchlin was well acquainted with Greek. Visiting Rome at that time, he entered the Greek academy, where Argyropylos was teaching. Reuchlin addressed him in language of condolence on the unhappy state of his native land. Argyropylos asked him, with an air of surprise, if he, a German, knew anything of Greece or the Greek tongue. Reuchlin replied by translating a passage of Thucydides, which the teacher had just been explaining to his pupils. "Alas! alas!" exclaimed the astonished exile, "poor Greece, like a persecuted fugitive, has gone to hide herself beyond the Alps!" Reuchlin returned to Germany, and settled in Wurtemberg, where he published a Hebrew grammar and dictionary; and by thus opening to men the long-closed treasures of the Old Testament, raised for himself, as he said, a monument more lasting than brass.

What Reuchlin had done for the Old Testament was accomplished by Erasmus for the New. Preferring to lead a homely and studious life at Basel, to either parading a cardinal's hat in Rome, or fluttering at the gay courts of Francis I. or Henry VIII., he published his first edition of the New Testament in Greek in the year 1516. It has been well said, "Reuchlin and Erasmus unsealed the Bible to the learned; Luther restored it to the people."

Martin Luther was born in 1483, seven years later than Leo X. His childhood and youth were spent amid poverty and hardship. In 1497, when Leo, already a cardinal, was enjoying the luxurious hospitality of Italian princes, on account of his banishment from Florence, Luther, a stripling of fourteen, trudged on foot to Magdeburg, and supported himself there at the public school, for some time, upon alms earned by singing on half-holidays under the windows of the richer townsfolk. After studying at Magdeburg and at Eisenach, he entered the monastery of Erfurt; and here, while the cardinal De' Medici was ambitiously scheming to regain the dominions of Florence, his future adversary was seeking, with agonies of earnestness, how he might secure the salvation of his soul. The one was encircled with luxury and grandeur, the other, in a dark, narrow cell, surrendered himself to abstinence, meditation, and prayer.

For a whole fortnight, on one occasion, did Luther endure such intense suffering of mind, that he neither ate, drank, nor slept. Often, on retiring for the night, he knelt at the foot of his bed, and remained there in prayer till the morning dawned. But the study of God's word at length revealed to him the way of salvation through Christ, and he then buckled on his armour to "contend for the faith once delivered to the saints."

Luther was still a Romanist. In 1510, he was deputed to visit Rome, to represent the case of some German monasteries to the pope. He was overjoyed at the prospect. The classical memorials of the eternal city made her venerable, almost sublime, in his eyes. And was she not also his spiritual mother? Was not Rome the fountain-head of pure and undefiled religion? So thought his unsophisticated mind. Alas! his sanguine expectations of delight were doomed to a bitter disappointment. His first surprise, on descending the Alps, was to find the monks of Italy so sumptuously lodged and feasted. They lived, he said, in marble palaces, and their fare was regal. Still he hoped to find better things at Rome. On arriving within sight of the city, he fell on his knees in devout ecstasy, exclaiming, "Hail, holy Rome!" He was quickly and cruelly undeceived. Everywhere he found dissolute manners, infidelity, and profanity. He visited many churches, and was overwhelmed with astonishment and grief at the indecent impatience which the priests discovered to get through the services. One day seven masses had been said before he could finish one. Another time, Luther was only at the Gospel when the other officiating priest had finished. "Haste you," cried the latter, "haste now, and have done with it!" "Get on, get on," said another, "and let our Lady have her Son again;" thus impiously alluding to the supposed transubstantiation of the bread into the body and blood of Jesus Christ. The licentiousness of the laity struck him almost as much as the profanity and luxury of the clergy. "This city," said he, in horror, "is full of disorders and murders."

From such scenes Luther returned, with a sad heart, to his German home. He was afterwards wont to say, "If there be a hell, Rome is built above it; it is an abyss whence all sins proceed. Yet, for a hundred thousand florins I would not have missed seeing it. I should always have felt uneasy, lest I were, after all, doing injustice to the pope." This visit to Rome was, unquestionably, one link in that wonderful chain of events, by which God bound Luther to the task he was destined to achieve.

CHAPTER XI.

Leo's prosperity and grandeur—His extravagance—Issue of indulgences—Albert of Brandenburg—Tetzel—Luther complains—Publishes his reasons—Tetzel retires in anger to Frankfort — Luther's opponents — Indifference of Leo — Luther's respect for the pope—Leo cites Luther to Augsburg—Luther's interview with De Vio—Luther appeals to a general council—Leo dreads an invasion of the Turks—Forms a European league—Marriage of Lorenzo de' Medici—Charles of Austria and Francis I. contend for the imperial crown—Charles elected emperor—Union in his person of many sovereignties—Death of Lorenzo de' Medici.

LEO had now reached the height of his prosperity and glory. He was firmly seated in power; his court abounded with witty and literary guests, whose presence added both to his amusement and his dignity; while the chief occupation of all around him was zealously to cater for his pleasures. He now amply indulged his taste for art, and liberally rewarded men of genius and skill. He gave large sums of money to the poets who recited his praises, and to the musicians who sang them. As eager to receive adulation as others were to offer it, he even courted the shouts of the populace, as some assert, by throwing a purse of gold daily among the multitude that thronged the gates of the Vatican. The profuse expenditure required to support so much grandeur, often compelled him to seek new methods of replenishing his exhausted exchequer. He was, at length, fatally advised to issue a general indulgence—a plan often adopted by former pontiffs, and which was never known to fail in producing a large revenue. A plausible plea was at hand. The church of St. Peter, begun under Julius II., was still unfinished, and the work was often delayed by want of funds. On this ground, it was determined to urge the liberal contributions of the faithful.

The indulgences which were issued on this occasion, impiously engaged that all who received them should be thenceforth absolved from all ecclesiastical censures and penalties, for whatever excesses or crimes, however enormous they might be, and from the pains of purgatory. They concluded with these words: "So that, at the moment of thy death, the gate by which souls pass into the place of torment will be shut upon thee, while, on the contrary, that which leads to the paradise of joy will be open to thee."

But the impious pretensions of these indulgences were surpassed in wickedness, if possible, by the scandalous methods employed to dispose of them. It was sometimes the practice of the popes to relieve themselves of the labour this trade demanded, by farming the indulgences to ecclesiastics of high rank, who would undertake to remit a proper proportion of the returns to Rome. The cardinal Albert, bishop of Brandenburg and elector of Mentz, offered to conduct the present business for Leo, on condition of receiving one-half of the proceeds. Leo accepted the offer, and Albert immediately set his creatures at work, to dispose of the indulgences at the largest possible profit. There was at this time a Dominican monk, named Tetzel, residing in Germany, who had been often engaged in this abominable traffic. He was a man of unblushing impudence, and so incorrigibly profligate, that for his crimes he had been once sentenced to death, and had only escaped through the interposition of a powerful friend. This man was selected as one of the agents for the sale.

It was in the summer of 1517, that Tetzel and his attendants entered the little town of Jüterbock, which was distant only four miles from Wittemberg, where Luther had resided ever since his return from Rome. At Wittemberg, Luther held the offices of professor in the university, and preacher in the town church. In both of these capacities he had already done much to prepare the way for his subsequent success. Although a Romanist, he preached and taught that salvation was obtainable only by faith in Christ. A large number, both of the students and of the citizens, had attached themselves to Luther, and strongly defended his views.

On Tetzel's arrival in Jüterbock, he set up a large wooden cross, painted red, in the public place, and mounting his pulpit, proclaimed the great boon he was come to confer. The people gathered to him in crowds from all parts, and, of course, among them were some of Luther's congregation, come from Wittemberg to obtain the pope's blessing. " Indulgences," said Tetzel, " are the most precious and sublimest gift of God. Come forward, and I will give you sealed letters, in virtue of which even the sins which you may have a wish to commit in future will all be forgiven you. Even repentance is unnecessary. But, more than this, the indulgences save not only the living, but the dead. The very instant the money chinks at the bottom of the strong box, the soul escapes from purgatory, and soars to heaven." After the sermon came confession, which was, in fact, only a chaffering between the salesman and the buyer about the price. The price was always governed by the wealth of the applicant, and ranged from five and twenty ducats down to half a florin.*

Some of Luther's hearers came shortly to confess to him. He was always accustomed to receive from them, not only a confession, but acknowledgments of contrition and promises of amendment, before he granted them absolution. On this occasion, to his astonishment, they avowed that they were neither sorry for the past, nor bent on improvement in future. They had received, they said, a plenary indulgence from the pope, and held up to Luther the document sold them by Tetzel. Luther indignantly

---

* The German ducat is now worth rather more than nine shillings sterling, and the florin about two shillings.

replied, that he made little account of the bits of paper they showed him, and added, "Except ye repent, ye shall all perish."

Luther now saw quite clearly the great guilt and mischief of these indulgences being hawked about for sale. He forthwith denounced the practice from the pulpit, and afterwards wrote ninety-five propositions respecting the doctrines taught by Tetzel and his associates, which he affixed to his church door on the 21st of October, 1517. These propositions may be regarded as the germ of the Reformed faith. The sixth teaches that the pope cannot remit any condemnation, but can only declare and confirm the remission of it made by God himself. The twenty-seventh, plainly alluding to Tetzel, says, "Those men preach human follies, who pretend that the moment the money chinks in the strong box, the soul soars out of purgatory." The forty-ninth affirms, that "Christians should be taught that the pope's indulgence is good, if the people do not trust to it; but that nothing is more hurtful if it cause the loss of piety."

Tetzel fumed vehemently at the publication of these propositions, but finding himself too weak to cope with Luther, he withdrew to Frankfort on the Oder, where he publicly denounced his antagonist, and burned his propositions. The news reaching Wittemberg, the students of the university retaliated, without Luther's knowledge, by publicly burning some counter-propositions, drawn up by Tetzel and his brethren. This served greatly to inflame the hostility of the monks to Luther, who, on his part, began to feel alarm at the prominent position he had assumed. But he was not the man to recede, and much as he would, at this time, have preferred a peaceful reformation of the church, his enemies were too bitter and fierce to allow of a reconciliation upon any terms. The fire was lighted, and the blaze now rapidly spread. Many advocates of the existing order of things started up to oppose Luther. The Roman censor, Prierias, spoke from the seat of the papacy, but his comments upon Luther and his publications were little else than a tirade of violent abuse. Hochstraten, a Dominican of Cologne, cried loudly for punishment on this unsparing denouncer of monkish hypocrisies and vices. "Let a stake be made ready for him immediately," said he. Dr. Eck, of Ingoldstadt, a warm adherent of the old scholastic theology, joined in the hue and cry, and although Luther had lately become his personal friend, promptly sacrificed the claims of friendship to those of interest and creed.

As for the pope, his education and course of life had not disposed him to care much for theological strife. He looked upon the whole affair, so far as he understood it, with indifference, not unmixed with contempt. "A mere squabble among monks," said he; "let it alone." When Luther's propositions were laid before him, he was annoyed at the presumption they displayed, but showed no anger. "A drunken

German has written them," he observed, sarcastically; "when sober, he will change his mind." Afterwards, however, Leo became an admirer of Luther's talents, and exclaimed, "Brother Luther is a man of fine genius." But he seems not to have entertained the slightest apprehensions of the danger that awaited the popedom. He had just escaped from a powerful conspiracy against his life, and the echoes of a tumult from so great a distance as Saxony conveyed no alarm. "We may now live in quiet," he one day remarked, "for the axe is taken from the root, and applied to the branches." Luther himself had hitherto held a very favourable opinion of Leo. "These days," he would say, "are too evil for such a man; we deserve an Alexander VI. or a Julius II." He often compared the pontiff to Daniel in Babylon, and applauded him for his agreeable and amiable temper. But, at length, he could see that Leo's forbearance was in danger of giving way before the ceaseless importunities of his antagonists, who earnestly prayed that he might be brought to trial for his heresies. In May, 1518, therefore, Luther wrote a letter of explanation to the pope, in which he expressed his willingness to abide by the pontiff's decision, whatever it might be. "I shall own your voice," he wrote, "as the voice of Jesus Christ, who presides and speaks by you."

Appealed to by all parties, Leo could no longer maintain silence; and, once compelled to adjudge the question, there could be no doubt which side he would adopt. His policy was that of his predecessors, to hush up inconvenient inquiry, and to silence every call for reform. His answer to Luther's letter was, a citation to appear before an ecclesiastical tribunal in Rome within sixty days; which, however, he modified a fortnight later, by permitting the examination to take place in Germany, and appointing De Vio, cardinal of Gaeta, to proceed forthwith to Augsburg, for the purpose of conducting it. The spirit inherent in the papal government, discovers itself remarkably in the instructions given to De Vio, when we find Leo, a mild and comparatively amiable man, thus directing his legate: "If Luther persist in his obstinacy, and should you fail to bring him into your power, we authorize you to proscribe him in all parts of Germany, to banish, and curse, and excommunicate all who adhere to him, and to command all Christians to shun their presence."

The conference between Luther and the legate took place at Augsburg, in October, 1518, and lasted several days. In repeated interviews, De Vio used every argument that might have succeeded with a weaker or more worldly man, to induce Luther to retract his propositions respecting indulgences, and the simple necessity of faith in the Lord Jesus Christ. By turns he pleaded and coaxed, grew angry and threatened—but it was all in vain.

Luther dared not give the lie to his convictions, and, to the astonishment of the legate and his courtiers, he persisted in defending all that he had written. After remaining in Augsburg for ten days, Luther wrote an appeal, "from pope Leo, now ill-informed, to pope Leo, when he shall be better informed," leaving it to be delivered by the legate to the pontiff; and, apprehensive that his further stay would expose him to tyrannical treatment from the papal envoy, he left Augsburg in the night-time, and by rapid and fatiguing journeys on horseback, found himself, in a few days, once more beyond the reach of danger, amongst his beloved flock at Wittemberg.

As he passed through Nuremberg on his return, he saw, for the first time, the instructions of the pope to the cardinal legate. It was the first glimpse he had obtained of the real feelings entertained towards him by the pope and the court of Rome. His indignation was greatly aroused, and he could not forbear from frequently expressing his amazement, "that anything so monstrous could have emanated from a sovereign pontiff." Finding, also, on his return home, that the pope, incensed that his legate should have been baffled, was tampering with the elector Frederic, to whose magnanimous protection he had hitherto owed his safety in Wittemberg, Luther resolved no longer to trust to the papal clemency or justice, but to appeal to a general council of the church. This he did, on the 20th of

November, 1518, and immediately afterwards published a protest, in which he boldly stated his reasons for adopting this course.

During these transactions, Leo's attention had been much divided by various political events, as well as by the ambitious schemes which he had long cherished in secret, and for the execution of which the fit time seemed to be near at hand. From the letter previously quoted, which he addressed to Henry VIII., it is evident that the advances of the Ottoman power gave him no little apprehension. The movements of this semi-barbarous nation had lately become more daring than ever. Selim, who now sat on the throne, was of a cruel and fierce disposition, and eagerly thirsted for foreign conquests. After directing his arms successfully against the Persians and the Mamelukes of Egypt, he turned his eyes westward, and all Europe was in alarm, not knowing on what quarter his vengeance might fall.

This general excitement appeared to Leo to present a favourable opportunity for uniting the European sovereigns into a league, for withstanding the encroachments of a foe, that was no less hostile to the ecclesiastical than to the political powers of the west. It was a favourite project with his predecessors, and Leo entertained it with equal zeal, to re-establish, by means of such a confederacy, the eastern empire, of which the pope might be the head. But, although the princes of Europe commended the design of the pope, and very readily entered into his proposal for a five years' truce among themselves, engaging also to defend each other against all aggressors, they were by no means forward to send the supplies that would be requisite, before any expeditions against the Turks could be safely undertaken. Still, the negotiations set on foot for this purpose were of benefit to Leo, and of yet greater profit to the agents by whom they were transacted. The cardinal Bibbiena, at the court of France, played his part with so much address, that he gained from Francis I. the rich bishopric of Constance, in addition to his other preferments. To strengthen the alliance between that monarch and the pope, he was also commissioned to propose a marriage between Lorenzo de' Medici, duke of Urbino, and Madelaine de Tours, one of the royal family. The proposal was readily accepted, and the marriage was celebrated with extraordinary splendour. Leo displayed his usual prodigality in the presents he bestowed on the bride. A train of thirty-six horses conveyed them to Paris, and among them was a state bed, composed of tortoise-shell, mother-of-pearl, and other costly materials. The entire value of these presents was said to amount to the immense sum of three hundred thousand ducats.

Another important matter had also occupied much of the pontiff's time. The young king of Spain was very desirous to be formally acknowledged as the lawful successor to the crown of Naples, which his predecessor had obtained by conquest. As Leo greatly feared, however, that the establishment of Charles's power in the south of Italy would give to that prince a dangerous preponderance of influence, both in Italian and in European affairs, he used every possible expedient, consistent with politeness, to avoid complying with his request. But, in January, 1519, an event occurred which altogether changed the aspect of European politics. This was the death of the emperor Maximilian, whose tenure of power had been characterized at once by overweening ambition and pitiable weakness. A contest immediately took place for the succession to the imperial crown, between Charles of Spain and Francis of France. That the former had the stronger claim there could be no doubt. He was a German by birth, grandson of the late emperor, and would in any case sway the sceptre of Austria. On the other hand, the peril was great, of allowing so much power as Charles would then possess to centre in one individual. On this account, and not from any love to Francis I., Leo earnestly supported the cause of the French monarch, at the same time secretly urging him, when the proper occasion should arrive, to forego his own claims, and to nominate instead Frederic of Saxony, or some other of the electors of Germany. But Francis was too ambitious to pursue so prudent a course, which would have had the effect of preserving among the continental princes a happy balance of power. He resolved on procuring the honours for himself, and endeavoured to accomplish his object by shamelessly bribing the electors. His ambassadors are said to have travelled into Germany, with trains of horses laden with treasure for that dishonourable use. But there was a yet mightier weapon in the hand of Charles. Finding that his rival was employing base means to insure success, he suddenly marched an army up to the walls of Frankfort, where the electors were assembled in diet. This bold step terminated the contest, and Charles was proclaimed emperor, on the 28th day of June, 1519, when only nineteen years of age. Thus did this prince, by an extraordinary concurrence of events, become the greatest potentate of Europe. Besides the now united kingdom of Spain and that of Naples, which he inherited from his grandfather Ferdinand, he received the Netherlands from his father Philip; the island of Sicily had long pertained to his family; and he now entered upon the dominion of Austria through the death of Maximilian. In addition to these extensive possessions, a second empire was in course of erection, by those Spanish adventurers who had followed Columbus to the newly-discovered world of America; so that it might be said of Charles v., as it is now said of the British sovereign, that the sun never set upon his vast dominions. So much power in the hands of a sagacious and ambitious young man, caused the monarchs of Europe to regard this youthful prince with a degree of respect and fear, which they were by no means accustomed to feel for one another.

The disappointment which Leo experienced in the accession of Charles v. to the imperial crown, was accompanied by another, which affected him still more severely. His nephew, Lorenzo, and his wife, Madelaine de Tours, both died in April, 1519; the former, in consequence of his licentious life while residing in France; the latter, in giving birth to a daughter, who was afterwards known as the infamous Catherine de' Medici. In losing Lorenzo, all the designs of family aggrandizement, which Leo had so ardently cherished and so sedulously cultivated, were blasted at a stroke. Had his plans been crowned with success, Leo would have eventually become the arbiter of Europe; but now that proud position was occupied by Charles v. The splendid visions of grandeur, which the pontiff had fondly indulged, faded away in a moment; and the vast power which he had hoped to establish in his family, while his hand closed upon it slid from his grasp, and was confided, by the " King of kings," to one who owed his eminency far more to events utterly beyond his control, than to any deserts or exertions of his own. Thus, oftentimes, is the ambition of vain man rebuked, and the lesson emphatically taught, that " promotion cometh neither from the east, nor from the west, nor from the south. But God is the Judge: he putteth down one, and setteth up another," Psa. lxxv. 6, 7.

The dominions of Lorenzo were now appropriated by Leo to himself. The government of Florence he delegated to his cousin, the cardinal Giulio de' Medici; the duchy of Urbino was incorporated with the states of the church.

CHAPTER XII.

Spread of Luther's doctrine—Leo anxious to conciliate—Miltitz—Luther's interview with Miltitz—Eck challenges Luther to debate—Disputation at Leipsic—Eck goes to Rome—Luther writes to the pope—The papal bull—Burned by Luther—Aleander and Charles v.—Diet at Worms—Luther's defence—His sentence—Rescued, and conveyed to the Wartburg.

THE attention which Leo had paid of late to the affairs of Italy had, in some measure, prevented his observing how rapidly that tide was rising in Germany, which was threatening to sweep utterly away the ancient landmarks of the Romish church throughout Christendom. Luther was every day extending his influence, both with the learned and with the common people, and the comparative quiet which he enjoyed for a time, gave him leisure to ascertain more exactly the true nature of his position; for it has already appeared evident, that this great Reformer had not entered upon his career of agitation with the set purpose of overturning the papacy, nor indeed with any definite plan at all. Gradually enlightened by the grace of God, he was often in painful doubt what course to adopt, and we find him ultimately rejecting many of the doctrines of Rome, which at first he had zealously defended.

The pope himself seems to have understood this much better than his advisers, and probably felt regret at the harsh measures he had been persuaded to employ. At all events, he was now anxious to conciliate the man against whom, through his legate De Vio, he had lately denounced the severest censures. It is not unlikely, indeed, that had Leo been left wholly to himself, he would throughout have pursued this conciliatory policy; for, although we often find him following the cruel practices of the times in the judicial treatment of criminals, yet there is evidence enough that his own disposition was comparatively amiable and mild. And it is not unworthy of notice, that Leo affords another mournful instance, that such qualities are quite compatible with a life altogether opposed in its spirit and principles to the holy will of God.

There was at this time a courtier dwelling at Rome, who seemed to Leo every way adapted to bring about a reconciliation between himself and the German Reformer. This was Charles of Miltitz, canon of Mentz, and chamberlain to the pope; a man conversant with the world, of polished manners, not bigoted to any creed, and, indeed, in all probability destitute of any settled belief. Him the pontiff decided to send into Germany, in the full expectation that, by good humour, flattery, and splendid promises, he would succeed in seducing Luther from a course, out of which he was plainly never to be driven.

Miltitz brought with him, as a present from the pope to the elector Frederic, Luther's protector, the consecrated rose, which the pontiff was in the habit of bestowing annually upon some prince, whose zeal for the church's interests seemed to merit so great an honour. This rose, fashioned in gold, and perfumed with musk, was accounted a symbol of the body of Christ, and was highly prized by the superstitious princes of that age, who looked upon it as a special guarantee of their eternal salvation. But Frederic the Wise was not to be decoyed by such fair-looking gifts. In consequence of Maximilian's death, he occupied, until Charles's election, the imperial seat, and he was conscious that this position gave him a most favourable opportunity of warding off from Luther the hostile blows of the pope. He accepted the rose very coldly, not even condescending to receive it in person, but directing it to be intrusted to one of the officers of his court. Miltitz, however, was in no degree abashed. He relied very confidently on his personal address for winning the Reformer back to the bosom of the church. Several interviews accordingly took place between them, in which Miltitz plied his powers to the utmost to induce Luther to retract. He flattered him on the popularity he had acquired. "Truly," said he, "I would not undertake to carry you out of this country, had I an army of five and twenty thousand men." He invited him to supper, embraced and kissed him, and with well-feigned tears besought him to "beware of raising a storm which might cause the ruin of Christianity." But Luther was immovable. He positively refused to retract, unless his errors could be proved to him. But he, at the same time, promised to abstain from further controversy, provided his opponents would do the same. With this limited concession Miltitz was, for the present, compelled to profess satisfaction, and meantime meditated other methods of gaining his object.

But even such an engagement as this was now beyond Luther's power to keep. He truly said, "God drives me onward. I am no longer master of myself. I would fain live in peace; but, lo ! I am hurried into the midst of tumults."

Dr. Eck of Ingoldstadt, the schoolman, had not ceased, from the time of Luther's publishing his propositions, to declaim against the new doctrines, or to denounce all who taught them. A vain and self-confident man, he was eager to come into collision with the Reformer, and measure his own strength with that of so redoubtable a foe, nothing doubting of success. Eck's chief antagonist hitherto had been Luther's disciple, Carlstadt; and in the course of controversy, a challenge was given and accepted, for a public disputation between them, to be held at Leipsic. But Eck was bent on dragging Luther himself into the arena, and to effect his wish, he published a series of propositions, in which that Reformer's doctrine respecting the primacy of the church of Rome was directly denied. Luther saw that he was personally aimed at, and considering that his compact with Miltitz was now broken by the pope's own partisans, he boldly took up the gage which the Ingoldstadt doctor had thrown down. It was arranged that the disputation should take place at Leipsic in the following June, and thus it happened that, while Charles and Francis were striving for political ascendency in Europe, these theological princes were contending with equal vigour for spiritual authority over the churches of Christendom — two memorable struggles, the consequences of which have remained to the present day.

There was a great gathering from all Germany to Leipsic on the 24th of June, 1519; for a public disputation was, in that age, a matter of as deep interest to the reflective Germans, as a tournament or a spectacle to their more frivolous neighbours, the Italians. Duke George of Saxony, the duke of Pomerania, the young prince George of Anhault, with a goodly number of nobles and knights, dignitaries of the church, from the bishop to the parish priest, and lastly, citizens of both high and low degree, filled the grand hall of the Pleissenburg palace on that exciting day. The proceedings opened with a debate, which lasted for two days, between Carlstadt and Eck, on the subject of the freedom of the will—a topic that has always proved too fertile of contention.

Then followed Eck's onslaught upon Luther, and the Reformer's spirited defence. The pope's primacy, purgatory, indulgences, absolution, and other questions, equally of vital importance, were discussed in succession, with much learning and no little acrimony. Quotations from the fathers by Eck were countervailed by Luther with quotations from Scripture. But Luther was more than a match for his opponent in even the patristic learning, and often convicted him of perverting or misquoting his authorities. In this manner no fewer than twenty days were passed, and still the disputants were unwearied, and the attention of the people never flagged. But excitement had been roused to such a pitch, that quarrels frequently occurred in the streets, between the partisans of Luther and the papists, as the adherents of the pope now began to be called. At length, on the 16th of July, the contest ended, without any public declaration of victory to either party. One of the most acute of the witnesses, Mosellanus, says, however, that "Eck triumphed in the eyes of those who do not understand the matter; but Luther and Carlstadt remained victors in the judgment of all who have learning, mind, and modesty."

Dr. Eck soon afterwards left Germany for Rome, where he hoped to receive much applause for the part he had acted in this disputation, and vainly supposed he should be able, from his intimate knowledge of Luther and the Germans, to suggest a method for effectually extinguishing the Reformation. Like Saul the persecutor, he " breathed out threatenings and slaughters" against all innovators on the established faith and worship, and was resolved to urge the most stringent and oppressive measures.

Miltitz was aware of Eck's procedures, and, burning with jealousy lest he should be outdone in the very business which he had been commissioned to arrange, he eagerly besought Luther to write an explanatory letter to the pope, which alone, he assured him, would be able to prevent Eck's obtaining from Leo a bull of excommunication against him and his followers. But Luther was now busily occupied in disseminating his doctrines. He continued to preach and write without intermission, and with so much effect, that not only Germany, but the neighbouring countries, were beginning to awake at the sound of the blows so unceremoniously dealt upon their long-cherished idols. However, in the autumn of 1520, he was prevailed on to write the letter, which it was hoped, by the advocates of peace on any terms, would have the effect of conciliating the court of Rome. Bitter must have been their disappointment on reading this important missive. Instead of retractation, apology, submission, it breathed the language of admonition, and even of rebuke, to the mighty prince who sat upon the throne of the church.

" From amid the fierce warfare," it began, " in which I have now for three years been engaged with unruly men, I cannot but at times look to you, O Leo, most holy father in God! And, albeit the folly of your ungodly flatterers has constrained me to appeal from your judgment to a future council, my heart has not turned itself away from your holiness, and I have not ceased to pray to God, in constant prayers and profound sighs, for your own welfare and that of your pontificate."

Referring to himself and his adversaries, he says, "I come to you, most holy father, and prostrate at your feet, beseech you to bridle, if possible, those foes to peace. But my doctrine I cannot retract. I cannot allow people to impose rules of interpretation upon Holy Scripture." Speaking of Rome, he says, "You know it, that, for many years, Rome has been inundating the world with all that could destroy both body and soul. The church of Rome, at one time foremost in holiness, has become a den of thieves, a scene of prostitution, a kingdom of death and hell."

Warning Leo of his dangerous position, he exclaims, " You, O Leo, are like a lamb in the midst of wolves, and like Daniel in a den of lions. Alone, what can you oppose to these monsters? There may possibly be three or four cardinals who are at once virtuous and learned; but what is that among so many? You would be destroyed before being allowed to attempt any remedy. It is all over with the court of Rome; the wrath of God has reached it, and will consume it."

Such language, uttered under such circumstances, must certainly be taken, not only as a satisfactory proof of the indomitable courage of Luther, but as strongly conclusive of the gross and general impiety of the Romish ecclesiastics. But, bold and true as the statements of this letter were, Leo was beyond reach of benefiting by them. Already, influenced by the arguments of Eck and others, he had issued a bull of excommunication; and Eck, delighted with his mission, was hastening to Germany to put it into immediate execution. But it was a great mistake in the policy of Rome to intrust this momentous business to the hands of Luther's most bitter foe. Everywhere the bull was regarded as Eck's rather than the pope's, and Luther himself affected, for a time, to treat it as a forgery. Moreover, during the interval that had elapsed since the Leipsic disputation, a great change had passed over the views of the Germans, both clergy and laity; and Eck found multitudes, on his return, zealous adherents of Luther, whom he had left warm partisans of the church. On arriving at Leipsic, he was forbidden by duke George to publish the bull; and his mortification knew no bounds when he heard the students of the university singing songs in the streets, ridiculing him and extolling his adversary. Receiving, at the same time, several letters threatening his person, his courage forsook him, and he was glad to conceal himself for the present in the monastery of St. Paul.

As for Wittemberg, he dared not approach it, but contented himself with sending the bull to the rector, accompanied with the threat, that if it were not published, the university should be destroyed.

Luther now thought the time had arrived for his taking a final and decisive step. Accordingly, on the 10th of December, 1520, a notice was placarded on the walls of the university, requesting the attendance of the professors and students, at nine o'clock, in the Place of the Holy Cross, at the east gate. A large concourse having assembled, Luther appeared, and approaching a fire that had been previously kindled for the purpose, solemnly threw into it the Canon Law, the Decretals, and other law books of the Romish church. Then, holding aloft the pope's bull, he exclaimed, " Whereas thou hast troubled the holy of the Lord, may the everlasting fire consume thee!" and then committed it likewise to the flames.

The war was now publicly declared, and the Romish churchmen were resolved on bringing it to a speedy conclusion. To accomplish this, they next had recourse to the young emperor, Charles v., to whom Girolamo Aleander was sent, as the nuncio of the pope. This man was well-fitted for his task, having no scruple at employing any expedient that seemed likely to forward his ends. On account of the talent he discovered, and the base purposes to which he devoted it, he has been compared to the Borgias, to whose patronage he owed his elevation in the church. He earnestly pressed upon Charles the necessity for Luther's writings being wholly suppressed, and urged that the Reformer himself should be signally punished, or at least delivered up to the pope. But Charles was unwilling, as yet, to do anything that might offend the elector Frederic, to whose kindness he was, in a great measure, indebted for the imperial crown; and he, perhaps, also hoped to find, in the person of Luther, a powerful check, to be advanced or withdrawn at his own pleasure, to Leo's ambitious designs in Italy. He, therefore, refrained from giving immediately any definite reply, and secretly determined that, at the diet shortly to be held, the Reformer and his opinions should undergo the examination of that august council.

This diet was opened in the city of Worms, January the 6th, 1521, and was attended by an unprecedented number of princes, nobles, and prelates, together with the ambassadors of foreign sovereigns, all eager to do homage to the young and powerful emperor. Many, also, had been attracted by the expectation that the great schism, which now distracted the church, would be a prominent topic of debate. The papal envoy, Aleander, had used every effort to convince Charles of the duty of pronouncing a severe sentence upon Luther, and the emperor at length consented that Aleander should bring the matter before the attention of the diet. Aleander was an eloquent orator, and, in a speech of three hours' duration, he gained over a large majority to the opinion that Luther ought to be condemned. But there were some who, though not friendly to Luther, felt, nevertheless, that the numerous abuses of the church called loudly for reform. Among these was duke George, who had presided at the Leipsic disputation, and afterwards forbidden the publication of the pope's bull. Standing up before an assembly, of which many were dignitaries in the church, he inveighed boldly and forcibly against the luxury, indolence, and impurity of the clergy. "We have a pontiff," said he, "who loves nothing but the chase, and other such gratifications; the church livings of the German nation are bestowed at Rome on artillery-men, falconers, footmen, ass-drivers, stable-boys, body-guardsmen, and such persons, at once ignorant, incapable, and strangers to Germany." It was finally decided, that Luther should appear in person before the diet, and answer for himself.

He appeared, in spite of the warnings and most earnest solicitations of his friends. "I will go," was his famous reply to all such intreaties—"I will go, though there be as many devils in Worms as tiles upon the houses." On the 17th of April, 1521, at four in the afternoon, he stood in the presence of the emperor, and the largest and most august assembly of potentates that perhaps Europe has ever seen. But he was without fear, though a solitary monk before powerful princes. He was strong in the sense of right. The officer of the diet addressed him, " Martin Luther, dost thou acknowledge that these books" (pointing to a pile of volumes on the table) "were composed by thee? Secondly, Art thou willing to retract these books and their contents?"

The titles of the books having been read, Luther replied, " I acknowledge these books to be mine; with respect to the second question, it is so grave, that I crave time, that I may reply without giving prejudice to the word of God."

No doubt, in asking this, Luther laid a tight rein on his naturally vehement spirit. He that day surpassed himself, proving that his conscientiousness could get the better of his ardour. His request was granted, and he was ordered to present himself the day following.

On the next day, business of another kind detained the diet till six o'clock. Torches were lighted, and this, with the crowded state of the assembly, made the heat most oppressive. But Luther spoke with his accustomed energy, first in German, and then in Latin. He concluded his address with the declaration, that, unless his opponents satisfied him from the word of God that his doctrines were untrue, he neither could nor would retract anything; "for," said he, " it is unsafe for a Christian to say anything against his conscience." Then, looking steadily around him upon that large and powerful assembly, from which so many fiery glances of enmity were darting at him, overwhelmed with the thought of his own impotence, he exclaimed, "Here I stand. I can do no otherwise. GOD HELP ME. Amen!"

The diet was filled with amazement at his temerity. Luther was ordered to withdraw, and a few days afterwards received permission to return home for the present. But his enemy, Aleander, worked so zealously and successfully, that, before the diet broke up, a decree was passed, commanding all the subjects of the empire to unite in refusing shelter to "the fool and madman," Martin Luther; to give him into sure custody, that he might be duly punished; and to burn all the books and pamphlets that bore his name.

Meanwhile, Luther, under protection of a safe-conduct from the emperor, was quietly pursuing his journey to Wittemberg. On the 4th of May, as the car in which he rode was passing through the gloomy forests of Thuringia, it descended into a hollow not far from the castle of Altenstein. Suddenly, five horsemen, masked and armed, issued from the wood, and commanded the drivers to stop. Luther's fellow-travellers, his brother James and his friend Amsdorff, took to their heels in great terror. The horsemen, seizing Luther, placed him on a horse ready saddled, and, riding off at full gallop, were soon lost in the dark solitudes of the forest. They took a circuitous route, turning and winding so as effectually to mislead any pursuer. Not till eleven at night did they cease their journey, and then they conducted their astonished captive up the side of a steep hill, thickly clothed with trees, to a castle at the summit, known by the name of the Wartburg. In this secluded and secure retreat, which Luther was accustomed to call his Patmos, the Reformer was detained till the heat of the pursuit was over. Months passed away, and rumour was busy in variously accounting for his mysterious disappearance. Spring, summer, and autumn glided by, and still he remained concealed; and, indeed, the hour of his release did not arrive till the pontiff who had set on foot, or at least authorized the persecution, was himself numbered among the dead.

CHAPTER XIII.

Discoveries in the east and west—Papal grants of territory—Leo patronises literature and the arts—Vatican library—Laurentian library—Sadoleti, Bembo, Aleander—Machiavelli, Paulo Giovio, Guicciardini—Bramante, Michel Angelo, Raffaelle—Poets of the age—Trissino, Rucellai, Sanazzaro, Pulci, Boiardo, Ariosto.

THE same spirit of inquiry which had produced such a vast revolution in religious opinions, had also stimulated research into all departments of philosophy and science, and, amongst these, mathematical and geographical studies were most sedulously pursued. Long before the time of Leo X., many discoveries of new countries had been made, and the Portuguese sovereigns had considerably increased their dominions by transmarine acquisitions. It was during the youth of Leo that Bartholomew Diaz rounded for the first time the Cape of Good Hope, called by that adventurer the Cape of Tempests; and he had not long reached the age of manhood when, in 1499, Vasco de Gama returned from his celebrated voyage, the first that an European had ever made to the eastern Indies. The last decade of the fifteenth century had also witnessed greater discoveries than these. In 1492, Columbus, seeking a western route to India, had caught the first glimpse of a new world, and, in subsequent voyages, had planted the Spanish flag on several of the West Indian Islands, and on the shores of America itself. From that period, the work of discovery was prosecuted by many European nations; and it is worthy of remark, that, although the sovereigns of Italy did not equip any expeditions for this object, many of the most distinguished voyagers, in addition to Columbus, were natives of Italian states.

If the princes of Italy generally had not profited much by these discoveries, they had not been without advantage to the popes. Accustomed to regard themselves as placed at the head of the universal church, they invariably claimed a right of interference in the disposal of the newly found territory. Were they not, they said, responsible for the spiritual welfare of the tribes that peopled these lands? Accordingly, Eugenius IV. had formally granted to the Portuguese all the countries from Cape Naon, on the coast of Africa, to the East Indies; and Alexander VI. had decreed, that all lands discovered to the west of an imaginary line, drawn from north to south, at a hundred leagues distance from the Azores and Cape de Verd Islands, should belong to Spain, whilst all that were discovered on the east of the same line should pertain to the crown of Portugal. In the year 1514, Leo X., following up in the new world the policy adopted by his predecessors in the old, made a formal grant to the king of

Portugal, not only of land already discovered, but even of such as were yet altogether unknown; accompanying it with the condition, that priests should be sent out, at the sovereign's expense, to convert the natives to the Christian religion.

But, whilst other sovereigns were engaged in enlarging the sphere of geographical knowledge, Leo, who had no navy at command, bestowed his chief attention upon literature, and encouraged both the recovery of the lost treasures of former times, and the production of new works, whether in poetry or in prose. He not only gave strict injunctions to his ambassadors and legates at foreign courts, to spare no labour or expense in collecting manuscripts, especially of the historical kind, but he sent forth numerous agents, with the express employment of purchasing from all countries these valuable documents, many of which are still preserved in the library of the Vatican. This library, founded by Nicholas v., was already become the largest collection of books and manuscripts in Italy. The officers who were chosen by Leo to superintend it, were always selected from among the most distinguished men of their time; and their efforts, no less than those of the pope, contributed to increase its stores, and enrich it with the choicest monuments of ancient wisdom and skill. Among its greatest treasures are some very ancient manuscripts of the Holy Scriptures, including, perhaps, the oldest extant, the celebrated *Codex Vaticanus*.

The library which Lorenzo de' Medici had so carefully collected at Florence, had passed through many vicissitudes. After the expulsion of the Medici, the Florentines sold it to the monks of the convent San Marco, and they, pleading poverty, offered it to Leo before his attaining the pontificate, for the sum of two thousand six hundred and fifty-two ducats. He gladly purchased it, and removed it for a time to Rome. Here he intrusted it to the care of the learned Varino Camerti, intending some day to restore it to his native city. Death prevented his fulfilling this intention, but it was accomplished afterwards by the cardinal Giulio, and was deposited in an edifice built by Michel Angelo, and still forming, as the Laurentian library, one of the principal objects of attraction to those who visit Florence.

Among the eminent names in literature that adorned the era of Leo the Tenth, some have been already mentioned. The two secretaries of the pope, the cardinals Sadoleti and Bembo, were distinguished for their skill in Latin poetical composition, an art which Leo greatly delighted in and liberally encouraged. Girolamo Aleander, the accuser of Luther at the Diet of Worms, was also a man endowed with remarkable talents, which he had industriously cultivated. From being a professor of the Greek and other languages in Venice and Padua, he was appointed by Alexander VI. secretary to his son, Cæsar Borgia. After the death of these notorious personages, he again devoted himself to study, and for his extensive acquirements was commended by Erasmus, and by the famous Venetian printer, Aldo, the latter pronouncing him the most learned man whom he knew. By Leo, Aleander was appointed librarian of the Vatican, and he afterwards rose to the dignity of the purple. Great as was his learning, his moral character will not bear a rigid investigation, and it is said that, in his last moments, he gave utterance to profane expressions of anger, because he was not suffered to complete his sixty-third year.

History was a department of literary composition which had now begun to receive considerable attention, and among the most eminent names of this period are those of the historians Machiavelli, Paulo Giovio, and Guicciardini. Machiavelli was a native of Florence, and, born a little earlier than Leo, also survived him. He belonged to the republican party in his native town, and, after the expulsion of the Medici, rose to offices of importance in the state. Consequently, when the Medici were restored, he was obliged to retire, and so reduced in circumstances did he become, that he would probably have languished out his life in poverty, if Leo had not called him to Rome, and engaged him in his service. His notorious work, "The Prince," was never designed by him for publication. We may further acquit him of sincerely entertaining the atrocious principles which it inculcates. Of these, his whole life, so far as it is known, was a practical contradiction, being spent in struggles for civic liberty. Poverty taught him to pander to the great, and it is a stain that will ever sully his memory, that he stooped to seek the favour of the Medici, by showing to Giuliano and Lorenzo, for whom the work was composed, that they might certainly become powerful if they chose to imitate the character of Cæsar Borgia, whose principles he there exhibits and illustrates. His history of Florence was the first work of that age which deserved the name, and, in the opinion of Hallam, is enough of itself to immortalize the author.

Paulo Giovio, or Paulus Jovius, is rather a chronicler than a historian. His voluminous writings comprise details of transactions in all parts of the world during his own time, but they are neither selected with judgment nor related with accuracy. Nevertheless, Leo, to whom he had presented some of his productions, was so highly pleased by his vivid and flowing style of narration, that, reading a long passage before a group of cardinals, he declared that, next to Livy, he had not met with so eloquent and elegant a writer. Giovio became a resident at the papal court, and was ever treated with marked distinction.

A far greater historian is Guicciardini, who not only related, but was himself a conspicuous actor in some of the most momentous events of the age. After filling with much credit the office of advocate to the consistory, he was appointed by Leo governor of Modena and Reggio, and continued in that and similar employments so late as the pontificate of Clement VII. His "History of Italy" is regarded as of pre-eminent worth, comprising every excellence that could be expected from a historian of that age.

To these, and to many others, only less renowned, the court of Leo was a secure asylum. It must, indeed, be confessed, that his patronage was not always most judiciously bestowed; the wit was too frequently preferred to the sage—the philosopher thrust aside for the buffoon. Ariosto, the poet, who graced the age, but not the court of Leo, was by no means solitary in his complaint, that, although the pope had often promised him large favours, on his coming to Rome he had only humbled his crest. The writer of an epigram would be repaid with a purse of gold—the author of an epic poem was forced to content himself with thanks.

In his judgment of the arts Leo was more discreet. He had been trained in childhood to admire the remains of ancient sculpture, and in the extensive collections made by his father, the taste of the young Giovanni had been fostered, in studying the same models that had elicited, and partially matured, the talents of Michel Angelo. The age of Leo is also distinguished for the number and excellence of the artists it produced. In architecture, Bramante, first patronised by Julius II., imitated the colossal magnificence of the Augustan age, and reared edifices which are still the glory of Rome, and of many other Italian cities. Amongst these, the cathedral of St. Peter claims particular mention, which, unrivalled as it is, has yet, in the opinion of some, been completed on a scale far beneath the grandeur of the original design. Bramante, however, only commenced the building, as he died soon after Leo's assumption of the papal crown.

The genius of Michel Angelo, also, has left but few memorials that can be referred to the reign of Leo x. This great master had all the proud independence and sensitive jealousy of control, which have so frequently distinguished and rendered unhappy men of a similar order of mind. By the peremptory Julius II., he was often compelled to labour at tasks to which he felt the strongest aversion. Having been requested by that pontiff to construct a sepulchral monument worthy to receive his remains, Angelo spent whole months in profound contemplation before tracing a single line, and then produced a design far surpassing in grandeur of outline, harmony of proportion, and variety of ornament, any that the world had seen. But the execution of the work was as tardy as the conception had been; and the now celebrated statue of Moses, with a few other figures, were hardly finished, when the vehement Julius grew impatient, and manifested his displeasure by treating the artist with supercilious neglect. This was more than Angelo could brook. He straightway left

Rome, and, heedless of five couriers sent after him in succession, retired to Florence. Subsequently he returned to Rome, fearful of too far provoking the resentment of the pope. Julius was still in an angry mood, and received him austerely, though secretly rejoiced at his return. A bishop venturing to intercede for the artist, the pontiff raised his staff, and bestowed a hearty blow on the prelate's shoulders, saying, at the same time, "Who told thee to interfere?" He then gave Angelo his benediction, and restored him to favour. On another occasion, the paintings on the ceiling of the Sistine chapel proceeding too slowly for his pleasure, he threatened Angelo that he would have him thrown from the scaffolding if they were not quickly finished. Under the fierce domination of this pope, Angelo saw that compliance was the path of wisdom; but under his milder successor, the sculptor determined to be his own master, and when requested by Leo to rebuild the church of San Lorenzo at Florence, he entered on the work so reluctantly, and advanced it so slowly, that, during the lifetime of Leo, it rose no higher than the basement story.

Nevertheless, there was abundance of genius in active employment under the patronage of Leo, and stimulated by the sunshine of his favour, Raffaelle, one of the most renowned men of that prolific age, gave to the world the ripest fruits of his toil. He excelled both in architecture and painting, but it is in the latter art his greatest fame has been won. During the pontificate of Leo, he was almost incessantly employed in adorning the chambers of the Vatican with the efforts of his pencil. To him, also, was intrusted, after the death of Bramante, the superintendence of the building of St. Peter's; and having received from the pope authority to guard from decay all valuable antiquities discovered among the ruins of the city, he devoted himself to the work with so much zeal, that he not only rescued many precious remains from inevitable destruction, but formed the design of constructing, from a survey of the ruins, an accurate model of the city, as it had appeared in the height of its glory under the emperors. But this intention was frustrated by his early death. It was also under the direction of Leo, who wished to hang some of the chambers in the Vatican with Flanders tapestry, that Raffaelle sketched those splendid designs for the weavers, which, after being cut into strips for that purpose, and thrown aside in a chest for many years, were purchased, probably by Charles I., and now form, as the cartoons of Raffaelle, the chief ornaments of the gallery at Hampton Court.

It will not be supposed, that in the general attention paid at this period to the cultivation of the arts, that of poetry was neglected. The age of Leo, it is true, was one of zealous imitation, rather than of original invention, in all departments of literature; but it nevertheless produced some poets, whose verse the world will "not willingly let die." Indeed, it has been asserted that Italy could, in that century, boast of no fewer than thirty poets, each of whom attained to considerable distinction. But, alas for the vanity of earthly fame! very few even of their names are now generally known, and those still held in veneration, with the exception of Ariosto, possess a very small circle of readers. The honour of giving encouragement and patronage to these men of taste and genius is by no means due exclusively to Leo. The princes of all Italy, stimulated by the example of Lorenzo de' Medici, vied with each other in rewarding labours, which many of them were very incapable of appreciating, and which they countenanced more for the sake of applause, than for any real value which they set upon intellectual or artistic skill. Thus the courts of Naples, Padua, Milan, Ferrara, Venice, and Urbino, were all adorned by the presence of men, more or less eminent in the various walks of literature and art.

The friends Trissino and Rucellai were the most distinguished poets who enjoyed the protection of Leo x. Trissino is regarded as the father of modern dramatic poetry, which he attempted to revive in the form of the ancient Greek tragedy. This servility of imitation crippled his powers, and his writings are now little valued. Rucellai, on the other hand, was an observer of nature, and in his didactic poem on "Bees," has invested a homely subject with much beauty, describing the habits and instincts of the little creatures in a very delightful and original manner. He seems to have regarded them with real fondness, and, by his truthful and life-like descriptions, inspires in the reader also a strong interest for them. In speaking of the civil wars of the bees, he thus pleasingly explains the readiest way of putting a stop to their battles:—

> "Delay not; instant seize a full-leav'd branch,
> And through it pour a shower, in minute drops
> Of honey mingled, or the grape's rich juice.
> Ere finished, you shall wondering behold
> The furious warfare suddenly appeased,
> And the two warring bands joyful unite,
> And foe embraces foe; each with its lips
> Licking the other's wings, feet, arms, and breast,
> Whereon the luscious mixture hath been shed,
> And all inebriate with delight. As when
> The Switzers, in sedition, sudden seize
> Their arms, and raise the war-cry; if a man
> Of aspect grave, rising, with gentle voice,
> Reproving, mitigates their savage rage,
> Then to them yields full vases of rich wine;
> Each, in the foaming bowl, plunges his lips
> And bearded chin; his fellow, with fond kiss,
> Embraces, making sudden league or truce;
> And, with the bounty of the grape o'erpower'd,
> Drinking oblivion of their injuries."

One of the most popular writers of this period was Giacomo Sanazzaro, the pastoral poet of Naples. His earlier efforts were in the Latin tongue, and he had written a long poem in that language, which he intended to dedicate to Leo, had not the death of the pope prevented it. He afterwards composed, in Italian, numerous elegies and sonnets, and one work of higher pretensions, a romantic pastoral, called

"Arcadia." In this poem, he describes the pursuits of the Arcadian shepherds, and represents himself as appearing among them, and relating his own history, together with the exploits and honours of his family. The kings of Naples, Ferdinand I., Alfonso II., and Frederic, loaded him with favours. The last of them presented him with the beautiful villa Mergolina, where Sanazzaro passed many years of ease and retirement, creating around him an Arcadia of his own. In the wars that drove the house of Aragon from the throne of Naples, Sanazzaro lost his estate, and the latter portion of his life was spent at Somma, a village on one of the heights of Vesuvius. Dying at the age of seventy-two, he was appropriately buried in a spot nearly adjoining the tomb of the poet Virgil.

But a totally different order of poetry, the chivalrous-romantic, was now much in vogue in Italy, and to this class belongs the greatest poems which the era we are contemplating produced. The marvellous legends of the days of Charlemagne had been favourite themes with the French minstrels for centuries past; and, mingled with equally wonderful incidents, derived from the stories of the Crusaders, formed a material which, to the ardent imagination of the Italians, seemed admirably adapted for the purposes of poetry. One of the earliest writers in this style was Luigi Pulci, who read to the critics assembled at the table of Lorenzo de' Medici, his Morgante Maggiore. This is an altogether extravagant narration of fabulous tales. The hero, Morgante, armed only with the hammer of a huge bell, crushes all that he encounters. The supernatural and improbable abound throughout the poem. About the same time Boiardo, a dependent on the duke of Ferrara, composed the Orlando Inamorato, a narrative drawn from the same sources as that of Pulci, but usually considered more attractive, from the variety and novelty of the adventures, the richness of the colouring, and the interest excited by the valour of the hero.

The undoubted chief, however, in this species of poetical composition, was Lodovico Ariosto, who carried the romantic epic to the highest point of perfection. Ariosto was patronised by Ippolito of Este, at the court of Ferrara, and was, on some occasions, employed in important political negotiations. The great poem which he has given to the world, the Orlando Furioso, of all the productions of that age, alone retains its popularity to the present day. The scene of the Orlando Furioso is precisely the same as that of the poems by Boiardo and Pulci. The sturdy struggles between the Christians and the Moors, in the reign of Charlemagne; the heroic prowess of the former, and the magical arts of the latter, are the themes on which the poet enthusiastically dwells. His narrative, indeed, is often absurd; the journeys and achievements of his heroes simply impossible; but, in spite of these defects, he contrives to excite in his reader the warmest sympathy for his favourite personages, and to delight and astonish with the pictures he so vividly portrays. In fact, Ariosto had drunk deeply into the spirit of the age of chivalry; and its faith in the marvellous—amounting oftentimes to gross superstition—its romantic valour, its devoted respect for the female sex, its exalted sentiments of honour, and its scrupulous performance of promises—are all faithfully transferred to his glowing page. His versification is distinguished for grace, sweetness, and elegance; and, in the opinion of a most competent judge, " the language is so perfectly harmonious, that no poet, either before or after him, can be, in this point, compared to him." The chief excellence, however, of this remarkable poem is the exact description it gives of the sentiments, opinions, and habits of thought, which prevailed in the south of Europe during the ages of chivalry. In this point of view, it is not only interesting as a work of genius, but cannot fail to awaken in the mind of the Christian reader the devoutest gratitude that a brighter day has dawned, and that while the better principles, traceable to Christianity, which were sometimes found among the heroes of chivalry, survive, and operate with still increasing strength, those remains of ancient paganism, which then lingered in the form of foolish superstitions, have altogether disappeared from actual life, and are only to be met with in old chronicles, or the imaginative productions of the poet.

CHAPTER XIV.

Leo's ambition—His treachery to Baglioni of Perugia—Attack on Fermo—Attempts on Ferrara—Designs against the French—Occurrences at Reggio—Invasion of Milan—Expulsion of the French—Leo's great joy—Sudden illness and death—Reflections on his death—Anecdote—Character of Leo x.—And of his age.

It had been well for the fame of Leo x., if he had spent the remainder of his life in pursuits as praiseworthy as the cultivation of literature and the arts. But the profound peace in which he had managed to preserve central Italy for the last few years, had enabled him so to strengthen his power at home, that he now felt tempted to enlarge his territories by the subjugation of the neighbouring states. Indeed, he entertained no less a design than that of driving both French and Spaniards out of Italy, and reducing the whole peninsula under the authority of the church.

In the general distraction of society to which Italy had been subject during the protracted wars of Charles viii. and Francis i., many of the petty states and weaker cities had been seized upon by successful adventurers, who ruled them, in many cases, with despotic and tyrannical severity. Such instances of usurpation afforded Leo a fair pretext for declaring war. Accordingly, the governor of Perugia, Baglioni, whose monstrous cruelties have supplied a theme to many Italian writers of fiction, was selected as the first victim of the pope's indignation, or cupidity, perhaps of both united. Pretending to be anxious to confer with him on affairs of importance, the pontiff sent for him to Rome. Baglioni, conscious of many crimes, and suspecting the pope's intentions, affected to be indisposed, and sent his son instead. Leo then assured him of a safe-conduct both in going and returning, and under this assurance Baglioni at length reluctantly complied. No sooner, however, had he entered the city, than, by the pope's command, he was treacherously seized, conveyed to the castle of St. Angelo, and, after undergoing the most cruel tortures, was finally decapitated in prison. The papal troops forthwith took possession of Perugia in the name of the pope.

Fermo, and the other cities in that district, were next openly attacked. The governors of some fell in battle, others saved themselves by flight, and a few, who, trusting to the clemency of the pope, resorted to Rome to implore mercy, paid the penalty of their rashness by suffering speedy execution.

Alfonso, the duke of Ferrara, had given great offence to Leo by the course he had pursued during the hostilities between the pope and the French king. Leo had never pardoned him, and an opportunity for revenge now presented itself, which he did not allow to escape. In the autumn of 1519, the duke fell ill, and was not expected to recover. Leo, therefore, caused his troops to march into the vicinity of Ferrara, so that they might be ready to seize on the city at the moment of the duke's death. In this plan, however, the pontiff met with disappointment. The marquis of Mantua interfered in behalf of the duke, and the papal army was withdrawn. Leo then resolved to employ stratagem and deceit. The year following, he sent an ecclesiastic, named Gambara, to Ferrara, who bribed an officer of the garrison, with a present of two thousand ducats, to open the gate of the city whenever the papal troops should appear before it. The army was in readiness, and the day for its admission was fixed. Even the plan of assault had been determined, when it was discovered that the officer had been merely playing with the pope's own weapons, treachery and dissimulation; for, whilst pretending treason to Leo, he had faithfully communicated to his master the entire details of the plot. Duke Alfonso informed the pontiff that he was acquainted with his meanness, and the latter, mortified and chagrined, was obliged for the present to relinquish his design.

Leo now felt himself strong enough to cope with the strongest powers in Italy, and determined on attempting forthwith the expulsion of those foreign aggressors whom he deemed most hostile to Italian independence. The French had long been growing unpopular with the citizens of Milan, and Francesco Sforza, the legitimate successor to the duchy, was impatiently waiting at Trent for some opportunity of regaining his inheritance. The pope, therefore, invited him and his adherents to take refuge in Reggio, a papal city, of which Guicciardini was then governor. At the same time, he made liberal offers to the Swiss, who engaged to furnish him with a large number of disciplined troops.

The gathering of the refugees and allies within the walls of Reggio gave natural alarm to L'Ecus, the French governor of Milan, and he quickly appeared before the gates, with the hope of surprising Guicciardini while he was unprepared to resist. But Guicciardini had received timely notice of his coming, and had taken every proper precaution, so that, when L'Ecus arrived, he could do nothing more than request an interview with the governor without the walls. To this proposal Guicciardini readily assented, and at the appointed hour L'Ecus approached, and dismounting from his horse, proceeded towards the gate, through which the governor passed to meet him. During the interview, a wagon, laden with corn, entered the gate, and a French officer, availing himself of the opportunity, attempted to introduce a body of soldiers. This led to a contest between the inhabitants and the French, in which the lives of both commanders were endangered by the discharge of artillery from the walls. By their united exertions the affray was soon stopped; but the affair coming to the knowledge of Leo, he represented it to the consistory as an outrage committed by the French upon his subjects, and thus throwing the blame of commencing hostilities upon the former, he immediately concluded a treaty with the emperor for assistance in carrying on the war, and issued a bull, by which he excommunicated both the French monarch and his chief officers in Italy, until Parma and Piacenza should be restored to the authority of the church.

By the month of August, 1521, Leo had assembled at Bologna an army of not fewer than twenty thousand men; and the arrival, soon afterwards, of the Swiss auxiliaries, so emboldened Prospero Colonna, the general of the Roman forces, that he marched directly upon Milan. The French commander, dismayed at the approach of so large an army, abandoned the other cities which he held for his sovereign, and shut himself up in Milan.

So intense, however, was the hatred of the citizens towards the French, that they contrived to convey intelligence to the papal general, that, on a signal being given, they would throw open their gates, and admit him and his troops. And so it happened; for, on the 19th of November, as night drew on, an attack was made, and those who defended the walls quickly yielding, one party of the besiegers entered by scaling-ladders at the point, and the remainder were immediately afterwards admitted at the gates. The French commander withdrew to Como, and Francesco Sforza was forthwith proclaimed duke of Milan.

The news of this victory reached Leo at his hunting-seat of Malliano. He immediately returned to Rome, and gave directions for public rejoicings to be celebrated for three days, with unprecedented pomp. Indeed, the joy he felt was far greater than the occasion seemed to warrant; but it was rumoured, and probably not without foundation, that the new duke of Milan had consented to exchange his duchy for Giulio de' Medici's cardinal's hat, which would have so largely increased the dominions of the Medici, as to render that family the preponderating power in Italy. It is painfully characteristic both of Leo and of his times, to find him, on this occasion, asking his master of the ceremonies, if it would be consistent with etiquette to return solemn thanks to God. It is too mournfully evident, that Leo's religion was much more the handmaid of political expediency, than the spontaneous offspring of his heart. Having given directions for the public rejoicings, the pontiff retired early to rest, not feeling altogether in good health.

The indisposition of Leo excited no apprehensions at first, and was simply attributed to a cold. But each day he grew alarmingly worse. He frequently complained of an internal burning, which none of the physicians appeared to understand, but which many have concluded was the effect of some poison secretly administered. It is said, that one of his cupbearers had presented him with a cup of wine the day before the indisposition appeared, and that Leo, having drunk it, asked him, in great anger, what he meant by giving him so bitter a potion. Others have ascribed his illness to poison applied to his linen, and not conveyed through the medium of food. Leo himself seems to have suspected treason, for we are assured that, with his last words, he declared himself to be a murdered man. He expired on the first day of December, 1521, in the forty-sixth year of his age, and the ninth year of his reign.

Sic transit gloria mundi! " Thus vanishes the glory of the world!" Such were the almost prophetic words formally whispered in Leo's ear, as he placed the tiara on his brow. How solemnly we behold them fulfilled! And what a commentary on the world's glory does the life of Leo present! Few have revelled in pomp and luxury more abundantly than he; few have "enjoyed life" so much, according to the world's estimate of enjoyment; yet who that regards life as a discipline for eternity, would not infinitely prefer the self-denying and suffering warfare of a Luther, to the ambitious and pleasure-seeking career of a Leo? Luther, sending forth to the world, and for the world's benefit, " thoughts that breathe in words that burn," from his solitary " Patmos," the Wartburg; and Leo, at the same hour, breathing his last amid the soft and silken splendours of the Vatican, the victim of secret malice, and stricken with dark fears of the future. How affecting and instructive the contrast!

Among the few memorials left us of Leo's dying moments, is one of an interview between him and his favourite buffoon, in which the pope gave heart-rending expression to the helpless agony of his soul. Of all the friends who used to flutter around him in the summer of his prosperity, not one remained to comfort him in the dark hour of death, except Mariano, the jester of the court. The rest had already abandoned the departing pope, to pay court to his probable successor. But Mariano, touched with his master's forlorn situation, and grateful for the many instances in which Leo had shown him kindness, continued faithful to the last. Compassionating, but unable to relieve the pain which appeared to oppress the dying man, more in his mind than his body, though the latter was suffering excruciating torment, the buffoon exclaimed, "Holy father, reconcile thyself to God." The poor pope, we are told, replied, as well as he was able, by sobbing out the words, "Good God, good God, O good God!" and thus his spirit arose to the tribunal of the Judge. How sad a commentary is this narrative upon those words of Christ, "What shall it profit a man, if he shall gain the whole world, and lose his own soul?" It was remorse of conscience that distracted the mind of Leo— the conviction that his sins were unforgiven, and that he was, therefore, unfit to die. We cannot forbear the wish, that, instead of the poor jester, there had stood at his bed-side some faithful Savonarola, but better instructed still than the Florentine in the way of a sinner's salvation. The years he had misspent could never be recalled; the talents he had abused, his wealth, power, and influence, were about to be finally withdrawn; but the Saviour, who soothed upon the cross the perturbed soul of the expiring thief, was still " mighty to save ;" and had Leo, instead of seeking to "*reconcile himself*" to God, been pointed to the " Lamb of God which taketh away the sins of the world," and sought to be reconciled through him, his faith in Christ's atonement would not have been rejected, and in the very arms of death he might, for the first time, have tasted, greatly guilty as he was, "the peace of God which passeth all understanding."

Independently of the conspicuous part which Leo acted in the transactions of those stirring times, few characters could be selected, that would better illustrate the chief features of Italian society at that period. It was an age of eager inquiry into all departments of knowledge, of keen relish for the beauties of art, of fearfully relaxed principles in morals, of impiety and infidelity in all matters pertaining to religion, of feverish thirst for exciting amusements and sensual indulgences. Leo shared, to a greater or less degree, in all these characteristics. If, on the one hand, he was not so debased as to descend to the depths of crime which others reached, still, on the other hand, his standard of morality was far too low to keep him wholly clear from pollution. As a pope, it is small praise to say that he is not to be classed with the infamous Borgia. He appears, nevertheless, to have been wholly unconscious of the vast responsibility which his position as ruler of the papal church involved. He did not scruple, any more than his predecessors, to barter professedly pastoral offices for gold, and thus to make base merchandise of immortal souls; while there is too much ground for the suspicion, that he did not himself believe the sacred truths which it was his professed business to diffuse.*

As a sovereign, he was, doubtless, more solicitous for the welfare of his people than many others of his time, yet he discovered no superiority to them in the avoidance of dissimulation and treachery; he was far more anxious for the aggrandizement of his family and the extension of his power, than for the happiness of his subjects, and on some occasions he was unquestionably guilty of cruelty and tyrannical oppression.

It would be uncandid, however, not to admit

---

* The writer by no means would be understood to imply, that he considers the doctrine of the papacy to be true, or its offices to be Divinely instituted. But, with the errors of Romanism, there have always been truths commingled; these Leo engaged to disseminate when he mounted the papal throne, and of these the fear is expressed that he did not believe them. That his moral responsibility increased with the increase of his power, although the basis on which that power rested was utterly fictitious, is taken for granted.

that there were redeeming points in his character. We have seen that he was generally more patriotic, more lenient, and more generous, than many who had previously occupied the same seat. His vices, though springing from the common root—the naturally corrupt heart—were, in their specific character, the vices of the age. But he merits the more positive praise, of having liberally fostered genius of most descriptions, and of having promoted, to an unprecedented extent, the cultivation of literature and the arts. By his patronage, the study of classical learning was astonishingly revived, and the native talent of Italy developed new strength, in productions that have assisted in enlightening the world. Leo was more prosperous than great, and perhaps more good-natured than wise; but he was magnanimous enough to give freely of what he had received, and sagacious enough, in general, to choose men of genius and talent for his friends. If we see little in him to excite admiration or esteem, we discover much to awaken our pity, and few will turn from the perusal of his history, without regretting that so much capacity and so many gifts, which, had they been consecrated to God, might have so greatly promoted his glory, should have been wasted upon trifles, or, at best, spent upon pursuits comparatively mean. The history of Leo impressively teaches, how vain are the highest endowments and the rarest accomplishments, except the soul thus ennobled has been animated by the breath of God's Spirit, and, having been "born again," has learned to walk in "newness of life."

The age of Leo has left behind it an equally valuable lesson, which the present and future ages will do well to study. We are far too prone to imagine, that certain men are quite necessary to the production of great epochs, and that, without a Luther, there had been no Reformation. But, to the attentive reader of even this brief narrative it will be obvious, that, if Luther and Melancthon, and all that noble band had never appeared, the Reformation was, nevertheless, a necessary event of the times. Had even the stubborn Hildebrand, Gregory VII., held the papal sceptre instead of the pliant Leo, the result must have been substantially the same. Luther and Zwingle might have died in the dungeons of the inquisition, but the Reformation would have survived. The light fell from heaven, and no earthly power could have prevented, or even have retarded, the breaking of the day. For more than a century, gleams of radiance had been fitfully flashing on the world—here in a Wycliffe, there in a Dante, anon in a Huss or a Jerome. Then, a more diffused and steadier, but still dim illumination, spread through society, and in Reuchlin and Erasmus, Wittembach and Lefèvre, we see the dubious expressions of the dawn. But earnest spirits are never wanting, and under the increasing provocation of a corrupt priesthood, the intenser manifestation that broke forth in

Luther and his associates, was an inevitable consequence of those laws of mind, which are under the sole guidance and restraint of Him, who " doeth according to his will in the army of heaven, and among the inhabitants of the earth : and none can stay his hand, or say unto him, What doest thou ?" To Him be all the glory !

www.ingramcontent.com/pod-product-compliance
Lightning Source LLC
Chambersburg PA
CBHW030820190426
43197CB00036B/689